Introduction

◆ ◆

This little book is designed to fit in a jacket pocket or a handbag. Once there, you are likely to find it very useful if you are the sort of person who likes to attend pub quizzes. Here's why.

The people who set pub quizzes have a habit of asking certain kinds of questions. There is a pattern to the way their minds work. *The Cheater's Guide to Pub Quizzes* tracks that pattern and gives you answers to the sort of questions that are most frequently asked.

How do we know they are most frequently asked? Simple. We set quizzes ourselves. We know it's done because we've done it. The *Cheater's Guide* is your way to beat the system. It provides you with answers to the most frequently asked questions in the most frequently asked subject areas. It's divided up neatly and logically in a series of user-friendly categories and has a quick-find index at the start of the book. When you want to find something in *The Cheater's Guide*, you'll want to find it quickly! No time for rummaging around.

We think you'll like this book, unless you're a quiz master. If you're a quiz master, you'll hate it. But for the 99.9 % of humanity who are not quiz masters, this book is your faithful friend, your old pal, your best buddy. Don't go anywhere without it.

C.H. D.Mac M. N.H.
Belfast, September 1994

Index

♦ ♦

Abbreviations

◆ ◆

ABM	Anti-ballistic Missile
ABTA	Association of British Travel Agents
ACAS	Advisory, Conciliation and Arbitration Service
ACCA	Association of Certified and Corporate Accountants
ADC	Aide-de-camp
AGR	Advanced Gas-cooled Reactor
AID	Artificial Insemination by Donor
AIDS	Acquired Immune Deficiency Syndrome
ANC	African National Congress
ANZAC	Australian and New Zealand Army Corps
APEX	Association of Professional, Executive, Clerical and Computer Staff
APT	Advanced Passenger Train
ARAMCO	Arabian-American Oil Company
ASA	Amateur Swimming Association
	Advertising Standards Authority
ASEAN	Association of South-East Asian Nations
ASH	Action on Smoking and Health
ASLEF	Associated Society of Locomotive Engineers and Firemen
ASTMS	Association of Scientific, Technical and Managerial Staffs
ATC	Air Training Corps
	Air Traffic Control
AVM	Air Vice-Marshal
AWOL	Absent (or Absence) Without Official Leave
AWRE	Atomic Weapons Research Establishment
BAFTA	British Academy of Film and Television Arts

BALPA	British Air Line Pilots' Association
BAOR	British Army of the Rhine
BBBC	British Boxing Board of Control
BCS	British Computer Society
BDA	British Dental Association
BEAB	British Electrical Approvals Board
BEAMA	British Electrical and Allied Manufacturers' Association
BEF	British Expeditionary Force
BFPO	British Forces' Post Office
BIM	Bord Iascaigh Mhara
BIR	British Institute of Radiology
BLMC	British Leyland Motor Corporation
BMEWS	Ballistic Missile Early Warning System
BNFL	British Nuclear Fuels Limited
BNOC	British National Oil Corporation
BOCM	British Oil and Cake Mills
BRCS	British Red Cross Society
BRS	British Road Services
BSA	Birmingham Small Arms
BSAC	British Sub Aqua Club
BSI	British Standards Institute
BUPA	British United Provident Association
BVM	Blessed Virgin Mary (*Beata Virgo Maria*)
CAP	Common Agricultural Policy
CARD	Campaign Against Racial Discrimination
CBI	Confederation of British Industry
CBS	Confraternity of the Blessed Sacrament
	Columbia Broadcasting System
CEGB	Central Electricity Generating Board
CFC	Chlorofluorocarbon
CIA	Central Intelligence Agency

CND	Campaign for Nuclear Disarmament
COHSE	Confederation of Health Service Employees
CPAG	Child Poverty Action Group
CPU	Central Processing Unit
CSA	Child Support Agency
CWS	Co-operative Wholesale Society
DDT	Dichloro-diphenyl-trichloro-ethane
DFC	Distinguished Flying Cross
DMZ	Demilitarised Zone
DNA	Deoxyribonucleic Acid
DPP	Director of Public Prosecutions
DT	Data Transmission
DTI	Department of Trade and Industry
EBU	European Broadcasting Union
ECG	Electrocardiogram
ECSC	European Coal and Steel Community
ECT	Electroconvulsive Therapy
ECU	European Currency Unit
EEG	Electroencephalogram
EFTA	European Free Trade Association
EMI	Electrical and Musical Industries (Ltd)
EMS	European Monetary System
ENEA	European Nuclear Energy Agency
ENSA	Entertainments National Services Association
EOC	Equal Opportunities Commission
EPNS	Electroplated Nickel Silver
ERM	Exchange Rate Mechanism
ERNIE	Electronic Random Number Indicator Equipment
ESA	European Space Agency
ESb	Electricity Supply Board
ESP	Extra-Sensory Perception

FAO	Food and Agriculture Organisation
FBI	Federal Bureau of Investigation
FET	Field-Effect Transistor
FIAT	Fabbrica Italiana Automobile Torino
	(Italian Motor Works in Turin)
FIFA	*Fédération Internationale de Football Association*
	(International Association Football Federation)
FIFO	First In, First Out
FM	Frequency Modulation
FOC	Father of the Chapel
FPA	Family Planning Association
FPS	Foot-Pound-Second
FRS	Fellow of the Royal Society
FT	*Financial Times*
GATT	General Agreement on Tariffs and Trade
GCHQ	Government Communications Headquarters
GIGO	Garbage In, Garbage Out
GKN	Guest, Keen and Nettlefold
GLC	Greater London Council
GLORIA	Geological Long Range Asdic
GUM	*Gosudarstvenni Universalni Magazin*
	(State Universal Store)
HCF	Highest Common Factor
HF	High Frequency
HGV	Heavy Goods Vehicle
HIV	Human Immunodeficiency Virus
HK	House of Keys (Isle of Man)
	Hong Kong
HMV	His Master's Voice
HNC	Higher National Certificate
HND	Higher National Diploma

HOLMES	Home Office Large Major Enquiry System (Police Computer System)
HWM	High-Water Mark
IAEA	International Atomic Energy Agency
IATA	International Air Transport Association
IBM	International Business Machines
IBRD	International Bank for Reconstruction and Development (World Bank)
ICAO	International Civil Aviation Organisation
ICBM	Inter-Continental Ballistic Missile
ICI	Imperial Chemical Industries
ICL	International Computers Limited
IEA	International Energy Agency
IEE	Institute of Electrical Engineers
ILEA	Inner London Education Authority
ILN	Illustrated London News
ILO	International Labour Organisation
IMF	International Monetary Fund
IQ	Intelligence Quotient
IRBM	Intermediate Range Ballistic Missile
ISBN	International Standard Book Number
ISEQ	Irish Stock Exchange Quotation
ISO	International Organisation for Standardisation
ISSN	International Standard Serial Number
ITT	International Telephone and Telegraph Corporation
ITU	International Telecommunication Union
IVR	International Vehicle Registration
KGB	*Komitet Gosudarstvennoi Bezopasnosti* (Committee of State Security)
KKK	Ku-Klux-Klan
kWh	Kilowatt-hour

LCM	Lowest Common Multiple
LDV	Local Defence Volunteers (later Home Guard)
LEA	Local Education Authority
LED	Light-Emitting Diode
LF	Low Frequency
LIFO	Last In, First Out
LILO	Last In, Last Out
LNG	Liquefied Natural Gas
LSD	*d*-Lysergic Acid Diethylamide
LSO	London Symphony Orchestra
LTA	Lawn Tennis Association
MAFF	Ministry of Agriculture, Fisheries and Food
MASER	Microwave Amplification by Stimulated Emission of Radiation
MCC	Marylebone Cricket Club
MCP	Male Chauvinist Pig
MFH	Master of Foxhounds
MHR	Member of the House of Representatives
MIDAS	Missile Defence Alarm System
MIRAS	Mortgage Income Relief at Source
MLR	Minimum Lending Rate
MOST	Metal Oxide Silicon Transistor
MRCA	Multirole Combat Aircraft
MTB	Motor Torpedo-Boat
NAAFI	Navy, Army and Air Force Institutes
NALGO	National and Local Government Officers' Association
NASA	National Aeronautics and Space Administration
NATO	North Atlantic Treaty Organisation
NBL	National Book League
NEDC	National Economic Development Council
NOP	National Opinion Poll

NVM	Nativity of the Virgin Mary
NYO	National Youth Orchestra
OAPEC	Organisation of Arab Petroleum Exporting Countries
OAS	Organisation of American States
	On Active Service
OAU	Organisation of African Unity
OECD	Organisation for Economic Co-operation and Development
Ofgas	Office of Gas Supply
Oftel	Office of Telecommunications
OPEC	Organisation of Petroleum Exporting Countries
OUP	Oxford University Press
Oxfam	Oxford Committee for Famine Relief
PABX	Private Automatic Branch Exchange
PBX	Private Branch Exchange
PCM	Pulse Control Modulation
PDSA	People's Dispensary for Sick Animals
PFLP	Popular Front for the Liberation of Palastine
PGA	Professional Golfers' Association
PIA	Pakistan International Airlines
PLA	Port of London Authority
PLC	Public Limited Company
PLO	Palastine Liberation Organisation
PLP	Parliamentary Labour Party
PLUTO	Pipeline Under The Ocean
PPS	Parliamentary or Principal Private Secretary
PRB	Pre-Raphaelite Brotherhood
PS	*Postscriptum*
PSBR	Public Sector Borrowing Requirement
PSV	Public Service Vehicle
PTFE	Polytetrafluoroethylene

PVC	Polyvinyl Chloride
QED	*Quod erat demonstrandum* (which was to be demonstrated)
QSO	Quasi-Stellar Object (quasar)
Quango	Quasi Non-Governmental Organisation
RADA	Royal Academy of Dramatic Art
RAOC	Royal Army Ordnance Corps
RAS	Royal Astronomical Society
RCM	Royal College of Music (London)
RCMP	Royal Canadian Mounted Police
REM	Rapid Eye Movement
RIA	Royal Irish Academy
RLO	Returned Letter Office
rms	Root Mean Square
RPI	Retail Price Index
RoSPA	Royal Society for the Prevention of Accidents
RSV	Revised Standard Version (of Bible)
RSVP	*Répondez, s'il vous plaît* (please reply)
RTE	Radio Telefís Éireann
RTZ	Rio Tinto Zinc Corporation Limited
SAA	South African Airways
SABENA	*Société Anonyme Belge d'Exploitation de la Navigation Aérienne* (Belgian National Airline)
SCUBA	Self-Contained Underwater Breathing Apparatus
SDLP	Social Democratic and Labour Party
SEATO	South-East Asia Treaty Organisation
SEN	State Enrolled Nurse
SERPS	State Earnings-Related Pension Scheme
SET	Selective Employment Tax
SHAEF	Supreme Headquarters of the Allied Expeditionary Force

SHAPE	Supreme Headquarters, Allied Powers, Europe
SNCF	*Société Nationale des Chemins de Fer français* (French National Railways)
SOGAT	Society of Graphical and Allied Trades
SPQR	*Senatus Populusque Romanus* (The Senate and People of Rome)
SST	Super Sonic Transport
STD	Subscriber Trunk Dialling
STOL	Short Take-off and Landing
TCD	Trinity College, Dublin
THF	Trust Houses Forte
THWM	Trinity High-Water Mark
TIROS	Television and Infrared Observation Satellite
TLS	*Times Literary Supplement*
TM	Transcendental Meditation
TNT	Trinitrotoluene
TT	Tourist Trophy
TUC	Trades Union Congress
TVP	Texturised Vegetable Protein
TWA	Trans World Airlines
TWI	Training Within Industry
UCCA	Universities' Central Council on Admissions
UDT	United Dominions Trust
UEFA	Union of European Football Associations
UKAEA	United Kingdom Atomic Energy Authority
ULCC	Ultra Large Crude Carrier
UMIST	University of Manchester Institute of Science and Technology
UNESCO	United Nations Educational, Scientific and Cultural Organisation

UNICEF	United Nations (International) Children's (Emergency) Fund
UNIDO	United Nations Industrial Development Organisation
UNRRA	United Nations Relief and Rehabilitation Administration
UPU	Universal Postal Union
UWIST	University of Wales Institute of Science and Technology
VAT	Value Added Tax
VERA	Versatile Reactor Assembly
VLCC	Very Large Crude Carrier
VRQ	Verbal Reasoning Quotient
VSOP	Very Special Old Pale
VTOL	Vertical Take-off and Landing
WASP	White Anglo-Saxon Protestant
WCC	World Council of Churches
WEA	Workers' Educational Association
WEU	Western European Union
WFTU	World Federation of Trade Unions
WHO	World Health Organisation
WMO	World Meteorological Organisation
WWF	Worldwide Fund for Nature
YHA	Youth Hostels Association
YMCA	Young Men's Christian Association
YWCA	Young Women's Christian Association
ZPG	Zero Population Growth

Bones in the Human Body

◆ ◆

Skull	22
Ears (2 × 3)	6
Vertebrae	26
Ribs (2 × 12 pairs)	24
Sternum (3 combined)	3
Throat	1
Pectoral Girdle (2 × 2)	4
Arms/Wrists/Hands (2 × 30)	60
Hip	2
Legs/Ankles/Feet (2 × 29)	58
Total	**206**

Skull

occipital	1
parietal – 1 pair	2
sphenoid	1
ethnoid	1
inferior nasal conchae – 1 pair	2
frontal	1
nasal – 1 pair	2
lacrimal – 1 pair	2
temporal – 1 pair	2
macilla – 1 pair	2
zygomatic – 1 pair	2
vomer	1
palatine – 1 pair	2
mandible	1

Ears

maleus	2
incus	2
stapes	2

Vertebrae

cervical	7
thoracic	12
lumbar	5
sacral	1
coccyx	1

Ribs

true ribs – 7 pairs	14
false ribs – 5 pairs	10

Sternum

manubrium	1
sternebrae	1
xiphisternum	1

Throat

hyoid	1

Pectoral Girdle

clavicle – 1 pair	2
scapula – 1 pair	2

Arms

upper arm	humerus – 1 pair	2
lower arm	radius – 1 pair	2
	ulna – 1 pair	2
carpus (wrist)	scaphoid – 1 pair	2
	lunate – 1 pair	2
	triquetral – 1 pair	2
	pisiform – 1 pair	2
	trapezium – 1 pair	2

	trapezoid – 1 pair	2
	capitate – 1 pair	2
	hamate – 1 pair	2
metacarpals (hands) – 5 pairs		10
phalanges (fingers)	first digit – 2 pairs	4
	second digit – 2 pairs	6
	third digit – 2 pairs	6
	fourth digit – 2 pairs	6
	fifth digit – 2 pairs	6

Hip Bones

ilium, ischium and pubis combined – 1 pair	2

Legs

upper leg	femur – 1 pair	2
lower leg	tibia – 1 pair	2
	fibula – 1 pair	2
tarsus (ankle)	talus – 1 pair	2
	calcaneus – 1 pair	2
	navicular – 1 pair	2
	medial cuneiform – 1 pair	2
	intermediate cuneiform – 1 pair	2
	lateral cuneiform – 1 pair	2
	cuboid – 1 pair	2
metatarsals (feet) – 5 pairs		10
phalanges (toes)	first digit – 2 pairs	4
	second digit – 2 pairs	6
	third digit – 2 pairs	6
	fourth digit – 2 pairs	6
	fifth digit – 2 pairs	6

Collective Creature Nouns

◆ ◆

Angel fish	Host
Animals	Menagerie, Tribe
Antelope	Herd, Troop
Ants	Army, Column, State, Swarm
Apes	Shrewdness
Asses	Herd, Pace
Baboons	Troop
Badger	Cete, Colony
Barracuda	Battery
Bass	Fleet
Bears	Sloth
Beavers	Colony
Bees	Cluster, Erst, Hive, Swarm
Birds	Congregation, Dissimulation (young), Flight, Flock, Volery, Volley
Bison	Herd
Bitterns	Sedge, Siege
Bloodhounds	Sute
Boars	Herd, Singular, Sounder
Budgerigars	Chatter
Buffalo	Herd
Bustard	Flock
Camels	Caravan, Flock
Capercaillie	Tok
Caterpillars	Army
Cats	Chowder, Clowder, Cluster
Cats, wild	Dout
Cattle	Drove, Herd

Chamois	Herd
Chickens	Brood, Clutch, Peep
Choughs	Chattering
Clams	Bed
Cockles	Bed
Colts	Race, Rag, Rake
Coots	Covert, Raft
Cormorants	Flight
Cranes	Herd, Siege
Crows	Clan, Hover, Murder
Curlews	Herd
Deer	Herd, Leash
Dogfish	Brood, Troop
Dogs	Cowardice, Kennel, Pack
Dogs (hunting)	Cry
Dolphins	Pod, School
Donkeys	Herd, Drove
Dottrel	Trip
Doves	Dole, Flight, Prettying
Ducklings in nest	Clutch
Ducklings off nest	Clatch
Ducks (diving)	Dopping, Dropping
Ducks (flying)	Flush, Plump, Team
Ducks (on land)	Flight, Flock, Leash, Mob Sail
Ducks (on water)	Badeling, Paddling, Sail
Eagles	Convocation
Eels	Swarm
Elephants	Herd
Elk (Europe)	Gang
Falcons	Cast
Ferrets	Business, Cast, Fesynes

Finches	Charm, Flight
Fish	Haul, Run, School, Shoal
Flamingos	Flurry, Regiment, Skein
Flies	Business, Cloud, Scraw, Swarm
Foxes	Earth, Lead, Skulk
Foxhounds	Pack
Frogs	Army, Colony
Geese (flying)	Flock, Gaggle, Skein
Geese (on land)	Gaggle
Geese (on water)	Gaggle, Plump
Giraffes	Corps, Herd, Troop
Gnats	Cloud, Horde, Swarm
Goats	Flock, Herd, Tribe, Trippe
Goldfinch	Charm, Chattering, Chirp, Drum
Goldfish	Troubling
Goshawks	Flight
Grasshoppers	Cloud
Greyhounds	Brace, Leash, Pack
Grouse	Brood, Covey, Pack
Guillemots	Bazaar
Gulls	Colony
Hares	Down, Drove, Husk, Lie, Trip
Hawks	Cast
Hedgehogs	Array
Hens	Brood, Flock
Heron	Scattering, Sedge, Siege
Herring	Army, Gleam, Shoal
Hippopotamuses	Herd, School
Hogs	Herd, Drove, Sounder
Horses	Harass, Herd, Stable, Stud, Troop
Horses (race)	Stable, String

Hounds	Brace, Couple, Cry, Mute, Pack, Stable
Ibis	Crowd
Insects	Swarm
Jays	Band, Party
Jellyfish	Brood, Smuck
Kangaroos	Herd, Mob, Troop
Kittens	Brood, Kindle, Litter
Lapwings	Deceit, Desert
Larks	Exultation
Lemurs	Troop
Leopards	Leap
Lice	Flock
Lions	Flock, Pride, Sawt, Souse, Troop
Locusts	Cloud, Horde, Plague, Swarm
Mackerel	School, Shoal
Magpies	Tiding, Tittering
Mallards (on land)	Bord, Flock, Flush, Suite, Sute
Mallards (on water)	Sord
Mares	Flock, Stud
Martens	Raches, Richesse
Mice	Nest
Minnows	Shoal, Steam, Swarm
Moles	Company, Labour, Movement, Mumble
Monkeys	Troop
Moose	Gang, Herd
Mules	Barren, Cartload, Pack, Span
Mussels	Bed
Nightingale	Match, Puddling, Watch
Ostrich	Flock, Troop
Otters	Bevy, Family
Owls	Parliament, Stare

Oxbirds	Fling
Oxen (domestic)	Drove, Rake, Team, Yoke
Oxen (wild)	Drove, Herd
Oyster	Bed
Parrots	Flock
Partridges	Covey
Passenger pigeons	Roost
Peacocks	Muster
Peafowl	Muster, Ostentation, Pride
Penguins	Colony, Rookery
Perch	Pack, Shoal
Pheasants	Brook, Ostentation, Pride, Nye
Pigeons	Flight, Flock
Piglets	Farrow
Pigs	Litter, Herd, Sounder
Pilchards	Shoal
Plovers	Congregation, Flight, Stand, Wing
Polecats	Chine
Ponies	Herd
Porpoises	Gam, Pod, School
Poultry	Flock
Poultry (domestic)	Run
Ptarmigan	Covey
Pups	Litter
Quail	Bevy, Covey
Rabbits	Bury, Colony, Nest, Warren
Raccoons	Nursery
Racehorses	Field, String
Rats	Colony
Ravens	Unkindness
Redwings	Crowd

Rhinoceroses	Crash
Roach	Shoal
Roe deer	Bevy
Rooks	Building, Clamour, Parliament
Ruffs	Hill
Sandpipers	Fling
Sardines	Family
Seals (elephant)	Rookery, Team, Troop
Seals	Harem, Herd, Pod, Rookery
Sheep	Down, Drove, Flock, Hurtle, Trip
Sheldrakes	Dapping, Dropping
Smelt	Quantity
Snakes	Den, Pit
Snakes (young)	Bed
Snipe	Walk, Whisper, Wish, Wisp
Spaniels	Couple
Sparrows	Host, Surration, Quarrel
Squirrels	Drey
Starlings	Chattering, Crowd, Mumuration
Sticklebacks	Shoal
Stoats	Pack
Storks	Herd, Mustering
Swallows	Flight
Swans	Bank, Bevy, Game, Herd, Squadron, Teeme, Wedge, Whiteness
Swifts	Flock
Swine	Doyet, Dryft
Swine (wild)	Sounder
Teal (on land)	Bunch, Coil, Knab, Raft
Teal (on water, rising from water)	Spring
Thrushes	Mutation

Tigers	Ambush
Toads	Knab, Knot
Trout	Hover
Turkeys	Dule, Raffle, Rafter
Turtles	Bale, Dole
Turtle Doves	Pitying
Vipers	Den, Nest
Walruses	Herd, Pod
Wasps	Herd, Nest
Weasels	Pack, Pop
Whales	Colony, Gam, Herd, Pod, School
Whiting	Pod
Widgeon	Coil, Company, Flight, Knob
Wildfowl	Plump, Sord, Sute, Trip
Wolves	Pack, Rout
Woodcocks	Covey, Fall, Flight, Plump
Woodpeckers	Descent
Wrens	Herd
Zebras	Herd

Computer Terminology

◆ ◆

Listed below are some of the most common computer terms used today.

ALGOL	Algorithmic Orientated Language
ALGORITHM	A plan/rootings for solving a problem
ANSI	American National Standards Institute
ASCII	American Standard Code for Information Interchange
AZERTY	The form of keyboard used in European countries so named because of the first six keys. QWERTY is the standard keyboard used in the UK and USA
BASIC	Beginners All-purpose Symbolic Instruction Code

BIOS	Basic Input Output System
BIT	Binary digit
BUG	Fault in a programme
BYTE	Unit of data/memory now taken to mean 8 bits
CAD	Computer-Aided Design
CAM	Computer-Aided Manufacture
COBOL	Common Business Orientated Language
EEPROM	Electrically Erasible Programmable Read Only Memory
EISA	Electronics Industry Standards Association
EPOS	Electronic Point of Sale
GUI	Graphic User Interface: another name for a WIMP system
KILOBYTE	Generally taken to denote 1024 bytes. Usually abbreviated to K
LAN	Local Area Network
MCA	Micro Channel Architecture
MEGABYTE	Literally, one million bytes but in computing terms generally denotes 1 048 576 bytes
MIPS	Millions of Instructions Per Second
MS DOS	Microsoft Disk Operating System
NEC	Nippon Electric Company
PADDLE	A form of joystick
PARK	Place heads of a hard disk drive over an unused track
PASCAL	Popular computer language heavily influenced by ALGOL
PC	Personal Computer
PIRACY	Unlawful copying of software
PSU	Power Supply Unit: source of DC power for a computer
RAM	Random Access Memory
ROM	Read Only Memory

SNOBOL	A String Orientated Symbolic Language
SQL	Structured Query Language
UPS	Uninterruptable Power Supply
USER FRIENDLY	Easy to work with
VDU	Visual Display Unit
VIRUS	A programme written to cause mischief to an operating system
WAN	Wide Area Network
WIMP	Window, Icon, Mouse, Programme
WORM	A piece of code inserted into a programme that will cause faulty or eccentric operation OR Write Once Read Many times
WYSIWYG	What you see is what you get

Entertainment

◆ ◆

Academy Award Winners (Oscars)

The year given in the list below refers to the year in which the award ceremony took place rather than the year in which films were made.

1951	Actor	Jose Ferrer (*Cyrano de Bergerac*)
	Actress	Judy Holliday (*Born Yesterday*)
	Director	Joseph L. Mankiewicz (*All About Eve*)
	Film	*All About Eve*
1952	Actor	Humphrey Bogart (*The African Queen*)
	Actress	Vivien Leigh (*A Streetcar Named Desire*)
	Director	George Stevens (*A Place in the Sun*)
	Film	*An American in Paris*
1953	Actor	Gary Cooper (*High Noon*)
	Actress	Shirley Booth (*Come Back Little Sheba*)
	Director	John Ford (*The Quiet Man*)
	Film	*The Greatest Show on Earth*

1954	Actor	William Holden (*Stalag 17*)
	Actress	Audrey Hepburn (*Roman Holiday*)
	Director	Fred Zinneman (*From Here to Eternity*)
	Film	*From Here to Eternity*
1955	Actor	Marlon Brando (*On the Waterfront*)
	Actress	Grace Kelly (*The Country Girl*)
	Director	Elia Kazan (*On the Waterfront*)
	Film	*On the Waterfront*
1956	Actor	Ernest Borgnine (*Marty*)
	Actress	Anna Magnani (*The Rose Tatoo*)
	Director	Delbert Mann (*Marty*)
	Film	*Marty*
1957	Actor	Yul Brynner (*The King and I*)
	Actress	Ingrid Bergman (*Anastasia*)
	Director	George Stevens (*Giant*)
	Film	*Around the World in Eighty Days*
1958	Actor	Alec Guinness (*The Bridge on the River Kwai*)
	Actress	Joanne Woodward (*The Three Faces of Eve*)
	Director	David Lean (*The Bridge on the River Kwai*)
	Film	*The Bridge on the River Kwai*
1959	Actor	David Niven (*Separate Tables*)
	Actress	Susan Hayward (*I Want to Live*)
	Director	Vincente Minnelli (*Gigi*)
	Film	*Gigi*
1960	Actor	Charlton Heston (*Ben Hur*)
	Actress	Simone Signoret (*Room at the Top*)
	Director	William Wyler (*Ben Hur*)
	Film	*Ben Hur*
1961	Actor	Burt Lancaster (*Elmer Gantry*)
	Actress	Elizabeth Taylor (*Butterfield 8*)
	Director	Billy Wilder (*The Apartment*)
	Film	*The Apartment*

1962	Actor	Maximilian Schell (*Judgement at Nuremburg*)
	Actress	Sophia Loren (*Two Women*)
	Director	Jerome Robbins/Robert Wise (*West Side Story*)
	Film	*West Side Story*
1963	Actor	Gregory Peck (*To Kill a Mockingbird*)
	Actress	Anne Bancroft (*The Miracle Worker*)
	Director	David Lean (*Lawrence of Arabia*)
	Film	Lawrence of Arabia
1964	Actor	Sidney Poitier (*Lilies of the Field*)
	Actress	Patricia Neal (*Hud*)
	Director	Tony Richardson (*Tom Jones*)
	Film	*Tom Jones*
1965	Actor	Rex Harrison (*My Fair Lady*)
	Actress	Julie Andrews (*Mary Poppins*)
	Director	George Cukor (*My Fair Lady*)
	Film	*My Fair Lady*
1966	Actor	Lee Marvin (*Cat Ballou*)
	Actress	Julie Christie (*Darling*)
	Director	Robert Wise (*The Sound of Music*)
	Film	*The Sound of Music*
1967	Actor	Paul Scofield (*A Man for All Seasons*)
	Actress	Elizabeth Taylor (*Who's Afraid of Virginia Woolf*)
	Director	Fred Zinneman (*A Man for All Seasons*)
	Film	*A Man for All Seasons*
1968	Actor	Rod Steiger (*In the Heat of the Night*)
	Actress	Katharine Hepburn
		(*Guess Who's Coming to Dinner*)
	Director	Mike Nichols (*The Graduate*)
	Film	*In the Heat of the Night*

1969	Actor	Cliff Robertson (*Charly*)
	Actress	Katharine Hepburn (*The Lion in Winter*)
		Barbra Streisand (*Funny Girl*)
	Director	Carol Reed (*Oliver!*)
	Film	*Oliver!*
1970	Actor	John Wayne (*True Grit*)
	Actress	Maggie Smith (*The Prime of Miss Jean Brodie*)
	Director	John Schlesinger (*Midnight Cowboy*)
	Film	*Midnight Cowboy*
1971	Actor	George C. Scott – he refused (*Patton*)
	Actress	Glenda Jackson (*Women in Love*)
	Director	Franklin V. Schaffner (*Patton*)
	Film	*Patton*
1972	Actor	Gene Hackman (*The French Connection*)
	Actress	Jane Fonda (*Klute*)
	Director	William Freidkin (*The French Connection*)
	Film	*The French Connection*
1973	Actor	Marlon Brando (*The Godfather*)
	Actress	Liza Minnelli (*Cabaret*)
	Director	Bob Fosse (*Cabaret*)
	Film	*The Godfather*
1974	Actor	Jack Lemmon (*Save the Tiger*)
	Actress	Glenda Jackson (*A Touch of Class*)
	Director	George Roy Hill (*The Sting*)
	Film	*The Sting*
1975	Actor	Art Carney (*Harry and Tonto*)
	Actress	Ellen Burstyn (*Alice Doesn't Live Here Anymore*)
	Director	Francis Ford Coppola (*The Godfather II*)
	Film	*The Godfather II*

1976	Actor	Jack Nicholson (*One Flew Over the Cuckoo's Nest*)
	Actress	Louise Fletcher (*One Flew Over the Cuckoo's Nest*)
	Director	Milos Forman (*One Flew Over the Cuckoo's Nest*)
	Film	*One Flew Over the Cuckoo's Nest*
1977	Actor	Peter Finch (*Network*)
	Actress	Faye Dunaway (*Network*)
	Director	John G. Avildsen (*Rocky*)
	Film	*Rocky*
1978	Actor	Richard Dreyfuss (*The Goodbye Girl*)
	Actress	Diane Keaton (*Annie Hall*)
	Director	Woody Allen (*Annie Hall*)
	Film	*Annie Hall*
1979	Actor	Jon Voight (*Coming Home*)
	Actress	Jane Fonda (*Coming Home*)
	Director	Michael Cimino (*The Deer Hunter*)
	Film	*The Deer Hunter*
1980	Actor	Dustin Hoffman (*Kramer vs. Kramer*)
	Actress	Sally Field (*Norma Rae*)
	Director	Robert Benton (*Kramer vs. Kramer*)
	Film	*Kramer vs. Kramer*
1981	Actor	Robert De Niro (*Raging Bull*)
	Actress	Sissy Spacek (*Coal Miner's Daughter*)
	Director	Robert Redford (*Ordinary People*)
	Film	*Ordinary People*
1982	Actor	Henry Fonda (*On Golden Pond*)
	Actress	Katharine Hepburn (*On Golden Pond*)
	Director	Warren Beatty (*Reds*)
	Film	*Chariots of Fire*
1983	Actor	Ben Kingsley (*Gandhi*)
	Actress	Meryl Streep (*Sophie's Choice*)
	Director	Richard Attenborough (*Gandhi*)
	Film	*Gandhi*

1984	Actor	Robert Duvall (*Tender Mercies*)
	Actress	Shirley MacLaine (*Terms of Endearment*)
	Director	James L. Brooks (*Terms of Endearment*)
	Film	*Terms of Endearment*
1985	Actor	F. Murray Abraham (*Amadeus*)
	Actress	Sally Field (*Places in the Heart*)
	Director	Milos Forman (*Amadeus*)
	Film	*Amadeus*
1986	Actor	William Hurt (*Kiss of the Spider Woman*)
	Actress	Geraldine Page (*The Trip to Bountiful*)
	Director	Sydney Pollack (*Out of Africa*)
	Film	*Out of Africa*
1987	Actor	Paul Newman (*The Color of Money*)
	Actress	Marlee Matlin (*Children of a Lesser God*)
	Director	Oliver Stone (*Platoon*)
	Film	*Platoon*
1988	Actor	Michael Douglas (*Wall Street*)
	Actress	Cher (*Moonstruck*)
	Director	Bernardo Bertolucci (*The Last Emperor*)
	Film	*The Last Emperor*
1989	Actor	Dustin Hoffman (*Rain Man*)
	Actress	Jodie Foster (*The Accused*)
	Director	Barry Levinson (*Rain Man*)
	Film	*Rain Man*
1990	Actor	Daniel Day Lewis (*My Left Foot*)
	Actress	Jessica Tandy (*Driving Miss Daisy*)
	Director	Oliver Stone (*Born on the Fourth of July*)
	Film	*Driving Miss Daisy*
1991	Actor	Jeremy Irons (*Reversal of Fortune*)
	Actress	Kathy Bates (*Misery*)
	Director	Kevin Costner (*Dances With Wolves*)
	Film	*Dances With Wolves*

1992	Actor	Anthony Hopkins (*The Silence of the Lambs*)
	Actress	Jodie Foster (*The Silence of the Lambs*)
	Director	Jonathan Demme (*The Silence of the Lambs*)
	Film	*The Silence of the Lambs*
1993	Actor	Al Pacino (*Scent of a Women*)
	Actress	Emma Thompson (*Howards End*)
	Director	Clint Eastwood (*Unforgiven*)
	Film	*Unforgiven*
1994	Actor	Tom Hanks (*Philadelphia*)
	Actress	Holly Hunter (*The Piano*)
	Director	Steven Spielberg (*Schindler's List*)
	Film	*Schindler's List*

Popular Music

Grammy Awards (awarded for record of the year)

1983	Michael Jackson (*Beat It*)
1984	Tina Turner (*What's Love Got to Do With It*)
1985	USA for Africa (*We Are the World*)
1986	Steve Winwood (*Higher Love*)
1987	Paul Simon (*Graceland*)
1988	Bobby McFerrin (*Don't Worry, Be Happy*)
1989	Bette Midler (*Wind Beneath My Wings*)
1990	Phil Collins (*Another Day in Paradise*)
1991	Natalie Cole, with Nat 'King' Cole (*Unforgettable*)
1992	Eric Clapton (*Tears in Heaven*)
1993	Whitney Houston (*I Will Always Love You*)

Top U.K. Singles

The top single for each year is that which remained within the top 3 for the longest period in that year.

| 1955 | Bill Haley & his Comets (*Rock Around the Clock*) |
| 1956 | Johnnie Ray (*Just Walkin' in the Rain*) |

1957	Paul Anka (*Diana*)
1958	Perry Como (*Magic Moments*)
1959	Cliff Richard & The Shadows (*Living Doll*)
1960	Elvis Presley (*It's Now or Never*)
1961	Elvis Presley (*Wooden Heart*)
1962	The Shadows (*Wonderful Land*)
1963	The Beatles (*From Me to You*)
1964	Cilla Black (*You're My World*)
1965	Ken Dodd (*Tears*)
1966	Jim Reeves (*Distant Drums*)
1967	Engelbert Humperdinck (*Release Me*)
1968	Mary Hopkin (*Those Were the Days*)
1969	The Archies (*Sugar Sugar*)
1970	Mungo Jerry (*In the Summertime*)
1971	TRex (*Hot Love*)
1972	Nilsson (*Without Love*)
1973	Sweet (*Blockbuster*)
1974	Charles Aznavour (*She*)
1975	Bay City Rollers (*Bye Bye Baby*)
1976	Brotherhood of Man (*Save Your Kisses for Me*)
1977	Abba (*Knowing Me Knowing You*)
1978	John Travolta/Olivia Newton-John (*You're the One That I Want*)
1979	Art Garfunkel (*Bright Eyes*)
1980	The Police (*Don't Stand So Close to Me*)
1981	Adam and the Ants (*Stand and Deliver*)
1982	Dexys Midnight Runners (*Come On Eileen*)
1983	Culture Club (*Karma Chameleon*)
1984	Frankie Goes to Hollywood (*Two Tribes*)
1985	Jennifer Rush (*The Power of Love*)
1986	Communards/Sarah Jane Morris (*Don't Leave Me This Way*)

1987	Rick Astley (*Never Gonna Give You Up*)
1988	Kylie Minogue (*I Should Be So Lucky*)
1989	Black Box (*Ride on Time*)
1990	Elton John (*Sacrifice/Healing*)
1991	Bryan Adams (*Everything I Do (I Do It For You)*)
1992	Shakespeare's Sister (*Stay*)
1993	Meatloaf (*I'd Do Anything for Love*)

Top U.S. Singles

1955	Bill Haley & his Comets (*Rock Around the Clock*)
1956	Elvis Presley (*Don't be Cruel*)
1957	Elvis Presley (*All Shook Up*)
1958	Danny and the Juniors (*At the Hop*)
1959	Bobby Darin (*Mack the Knife*)
1960	Percy Faith (The Theme from '*A Summer Place*')
1961	Bobby Lewis (*Tossin' and Turnin'*)
1962	Ray Charles (*I Can't Stop Loving You*)
1963	Jimmy Gilmer and the Fireballs (*Sugar Shack*)
1964	The Beatles (*I Want to Hold Your Hand*)
1965	Rolling Stones (*(I Can't Get No) Satisfaction*)
1966	The Monkees (*I'm a Believer*)
1967	Lulu (*To Sir with Love*)
1968	The Beatles (*Hey Jude*)
1969	5th Dimension (*Aquarius/Let the Sunshine In*)
1970	Simon and Garfunkel (*Bridge over Troubled Waters*)
1971	Three Dog Night (*Joy to the World*)
1972	Roberta Flack (*The First Time Ever I Saw Your Face*)
1973	Roberta Flack (*Killing me Softly with his Song*)
1974	Barbra Streisand (*The Way We Were*)
1975	Captain and Tennille (*Love will Keep us Together*)
1976	Rod Stewart (*Tonight's the Night*)

1977   Debby Boone (*You Light up my Life*)

1978   Bee Gees (*Night Fever*)

1979   The Knack (*My Sharona*)

1980   Kenny Rogers (*Lady*)

1981   Olivia Newton-John (*Physical*)

1982   Joan Jett and the Blackhearts (*I Love Rock 'n' Roll*)

1983   The Police (*Every Breath You Take*)

1984   Madonna (*Like a Virgin*)

1985   Lionel Richie (*Say You, Say Me*)

1986   Dionne and Friends (*That's What Friends Are For*)

1987   George Michael (*Faith*)

1988   Steve Winwood (*Roll With It*)

1989   Phil Collins (*Another Day in Paradise*)

1990   Mariah Carey (*Vision of Love*)

1991   Bryan Adams (*Everything I Do (I Do It For You)*)

1992   Sir Mix-a-lot (*Baby Got Back*)

1993   Tag Team (*Whoomp There It Is*)

Entertainers' Real Names

Allen, Dave	David Tynan O'Mahoney
Allen, Woody	Allen Stewart Konigsberg
Andrews, Julie	Julia Elizabeth Wells
Ant, Adam	Stuart Goddard
Astaire, Fred	Frederick Austerlitz
Atlas, Charles	Angelo Siciliano
Bacall, Lauren	Betty Joan Perske
Ball, Lucille	Lucille Hunt
Bancroft, Anne	Anna Maria Italiano
Bara, Theda	Theodosia Goodman
Bardot, Brigitte	Camille Javal
Benny, Jack	Benjamin Kubelsky

Berlin, Irving	Israel Baline
Bolan, Marc	Marc Feld
Bowie, David	David Hayward Jones
Brett, Jeremy	Peter Jeremy Huggins
Bronson, Charles	Charles Buchinski
Brooks, Elkie	Elaine Bookbinder
Brooks, Mel	Melvin Kaminsky
Burns, George	Nathan Birnbaum
Burton, Richard	Richard Walter Jenkins
Caine, Marti	Lynda Crapper
Caine, Michael	Maurice Micklewhite
Carrott, Jasper	Robert Davies
Chandler, Jeff	Ira Grossel
Charisse, Cyd	Tula Finklea
Cher	Cherilyn Sarkisian Lapierre
Clapton, Eric	Eric Clapp
Como, Perry	Nick Perido
Crawford, Joan	Lucille La Sueur
Crawford, Michael	Michael Dumble-Smith
Curtis, Tony	Bernard Schwartz
Darin, Bobby	Walden Robert Cassotto
Dean, James	James Byron
Dee, Kiki	Pauline Matthews
Diamond, Neil	Noah Kaminsky
Everett, Kenny	Maurice Cole
Faith, Adam	Terence Nelhams
Fame, Georgie	Clive Powell
Fields, W.C.	William Claude Dukinfield
Forsyth, Bruce	Bruce Johnson
Fury, Billy	Ronald Wycherly
Garland, Judy	Frances Ethel Gumm

Garner, James	James Baumgartner
George, Boy	George O'Dowd
Glitter, Gary	Paul Gadd
Grayson, Larry	William White
Harvey, Laurence	Larushka Mischa Skikne
Hayworth, Rita	Marguerita Cansino
Heston, Charlton	Charlton Carter
Houdini, Harry	Erik Weisz
John, Elton	Reginald Kenneth Dwight
Jones, Tom	Thomas Woodward
Karloff, Boris	William Pratt
Kaye, Danny	David Daniel Kaminsky
Large, Eddie	Edward McGinnis
Laurel, Stan	Arthur Stanley Jefferson
Lee, Peggy	Norma Egstrom
Lewis, Jerry	Jerry Levitch
Little, Sid	Cyril John Mead
Madonna	Madonna Louise Ciccone
Mann, Manfred	Michael Lubowitz
Meatloaf	Marvin Lee Aday
Mercury, Freddie	Frederick Bulsara
Morecambe, Eric	Eric Bartholomew
O'Hara, Maureen	Maureen Fitzsimmons
Pallo, Jackie	John Gutteridge
Prince	Prince Rogers Nelson
Rogers, Ginger	Virginia Katharine McMath
Rogers, Roy	Leonard Slye
Rooney, Mickey	Joe Yule Jr.
Rotten, Johnny	John Lydon
Sharif, Omar	Michel Shalhoub
Stardust, Alvin	Bernard William Jewry

Steele, Tommy	Thomas Hicks
Stevens, Cat	Steven Giorgiou
Sting	Gordon Sumner
Turner, Tina	Annie Mae Bullock
Vaughan, Frankie	Frank Abelsohn
Wilde, Marty	Reginald Smith
Windsor, Barbara	Barbara Anne Deeks
Wonder, Stevie	Stephen Judkins
Wyman, Bill	William Perks

Popular Characters in TV Soaps

Coronation Street

Bet Gilroy	Julie Goodyear
Raquel Wolstenholme	Sarah Lancashire
Des Barnes	Philip Middlemiss
Derek Wilton	Peter Baldwin
Mavis Wilton	Thelma Barlow
Emily Bishop	Eileen Derbyshire
Mike Baldwin	Johnny Briggs
Alma Baldwin	Amanda Barrie
Jim McDonald	Charles Lawson
Betty Turpin	Betty Driver
Ken Barlow	William Roache
Jack Duckworth	Bill Tarmey
Vera Duckworth	Elizabeth Dawn

Eastenders

Pauline	Wendy Richard
Frank	Mike Reid
Kathy	Gillian Taylforth
Cindy	Michelle Collins
Michelle	Susan Tully

Grant	Ross Kemp
Arthur	Bill Treacher
Ian	Adam Woodyatt
Pat	Pam St Clement
Natalie	Lucy Speed
Phil	Steve McFadden
Nellie	Elizabeth Kelly
Steve	Mark Mowera

Emmerdale Farm

Frank Tate	Norman Bowler
Joe Sugden	Frazier Hines
Jack Sugden	Clive Hornby
Seth Armstrong	Stan Richards
Kim Barker	Clare King
Shirely Turner	Rachel Davies
Elsa Feldman	Naomi Lewis
Christopher Tate	Peter Amory
Rachel Hughes	Glenda McKay

Neighbours

Jim Robinson	Alan Dale
Helen Daniels	Anne Haddy
Doug Wallis	Terence Donovan
Pam Willis	Sue Jones
Brad Willis	Scott Michaelson
Lou Carpenter	Tom Oliver
Lauren Carpenter	Sarah Vandenberg
Cameron Hudson	Benjamin Mitchell
Beth Brennan	Natalie Imbruglia
Benito Alessi	George Spatels

Cathy Alessi   Elspeth Ballantyne
Rick Alessi   Dan Falzon

Home and Away
Adam   Mat Stevenson
Shane   Deiter Brummen
Michael   Denis Coard
Fisher   Norman Coburn
Damien   Matt Doran
Roxanne   Lisa Lackey
Alf   Ray Meagher

Brookside
Jimmy Corkhill   Dean Sullivan
Jackie Corkhill   Sue Jenkins
D.D. Dixon   Irene Maron
Jaqui Dixon   Alexandra Fletcher
David Crosby   John Burgess
Penny Crosby   Mary Tamm
Jean Crosbie   Marcia Ashton
Mandy Jordache   Sandra Maitland
Beth Jordache   Anna Friel
Carol Salter   Angela Walsh
Garry Salter   Steven Dwyer
Mick Johnson   Louis Emerick

Glenroe
Dinny Byrne   Joe Lynch
Miley Byrne   Mick Lally
Biddy Byrne   Mary McEvoy
Mary McDermott–Moran   Geraldine Plunkett
Dick Moran   Emmet Bergin

Stephen Brennan	Robert Carrickford
Teasie McDaid	Maureen Toal
Michelle Haughey	Isobel Mahon
Fiona March–Black	Lucy Vigne Welsh
Mick Killeen	Gerry Sullivan
Rev George Black	Enda Oates
Rory Dolan	Andrew Roddy
Judy Stewart	Pauline Hutton
Marjorie Vincent	Leslie Lalor

The Bill

DCI Meadows	Simon Rouse
Brian Linton	David Haig
Sgt Boyden	Tony O'Callaghan
DC Woods	Tom Cotcher
PC Ackland	Trudie Goodwin
PC Loxton	Tom Butcher
Chief Insp Cato	Phillip Whitchurch
Insp Munroe	Colin Tarrant
Sgt Steele	Robert Perkins
PC Jarvis	Stephen Beckett

Geography

The information given in this section has been compiled from *The Times Atlas of the World*. Slightly different figures may be found in other reference books.

◆ ◆

Oceans	Area (km^2/miles^2)
Pacific	63 838 000/165 384 000
Atlantic	31 736 000/82 217 000
Indian	28 364 000/73 481 000
Arctic	5 426 000/14 056 000

Largest Seas	Area (km^2/miles^2)
Mediterranean Sea	967 000/2 505 000
South China Sea	895 000/2 318 000
Bering Sea	876 000/2 269 000
Caribbean Sea	750 000/1 943 000
Gulf of Mexico	596 000/1 544 000

Longest Rivers	Length (km/miles)
Nile (Africa)	6695/4160
Amazon (S Amer)	6516/4050
Yangtze (*Chang Jiang*) (Asia)	6380/3965
Mississippi-Missouri (N Amer)	6019/3740
Ob'-Irtysh (Asia)	5570/3460
Yenisey-Angara (Asia)	5550/3450
Hwang He (*Yellow River*) (Asia)	5464/3395
Zaire (*Congo*) (Africa)	4667/2900
Paraná (S Amer)	4500/2800
Mekong (Asia)	4425/2750
Amur (*Heilongjiang*) (Asia)	4416/2744
Lena (Asia)	4400/2730
Mackenzie (N Amer)	4250/2640
Niger (Africa)	4030/2505
Murray-Darling (Australasia)	3750/2330

Largest Lakes	Area (km^2/miles^2)
Caspian Sea (Asia)	371 000/143 205
Lake Superior (N Amer)	83 270/32 140
Lake Victoria (Nyanza) (Africa)	68 800/26 560
Aral Sea (Asia)	65 500/25 285
Lake Huron (N Amer)	60 700/23 430
Lake Michigan (N Amer)	58 020/22 395

Lake Tanganyika (Africa)	32 900/13 860
Great Bear Lake (N Amer)	31 790/12 270
Lake Baikal (Asia)	30 500/11 775
Lake Malawi (Africa)	22 490/8 680

Largest Deserts	Approx. area (km^2/$miles^2$)
Sahara (Africa)	8 400 000/3 250 000
Australian Desert (Australia)	1 550 000/600 000
Arabian Desert (Arabian Peninsula)	1 300 000/500 000
Gobi Desert (Mongolia/China)	1 040 000/400 000
Kalahari Desert (Botswana)	520 000/200 000
Takla Makan (China)	320 000/125 000
Sonoran Desert (USA/Mexico)	310 000/120 000
Namib Desert (Namibia)	310 000/120 000
Kara Kum (Kazakhstan)	270 000/105 000
Thar Desert (India/Pakistan)	260 000/100 000
Somali Desert (Somalia)	260 000/100 000
Atacama Desert (Chile)	180 000/70 000
Kyzyl Kum (Kazakhstan)	180 000/70 000
Dasht-e Lut (salt waste—Iran)	52 000/20 000
Mojave Desert (USA)	35 000/13 500
Desierto de Sechura (Peru)	26 000/10 000

Highest Mountains	Height (m/ft)
Mount Everest (China/Nepal)	8848/29 028
K2 (Kashmir/China)	8611/28 250
Kangchenjunga (India/Nepal)	8586/28 170
Lhotse (China/Nepal)	8516/27 939
Makalu 1 (China/Nepal)	8463/27 766
in North America: Mount McKinley (USA)	6194/20 320
in South America: Aconcagua (Argentina)	6960/22 834
in Africa: Kilimanjaro (Tanzania)	5895/19 340
in Europe: Mont Blanc (France/Italy)	4807/15 770

Largest Islands	Approx. area ($km^2/miles^2$)
Greenland (Arctic Ocean)	2 175 600/839 780
New Guinea (Pacific Ocean)	808 510/312 085
Borneo (Indian Ocean)	757 050/292 220
Madagascar (Indian Ocean)	594 180/229 355
Sumatra (Indian Ocean)	524 100/202 300
Baffin Island (Arctic Ocean)	476 070/183 760
Honshu (Pacific Ocean)	230 455/88 955
Great Britain (Atlantic Ocean)	229 870/88730
Ellesmere Island (Arctic Ocean)	212 690/82 100
Victoria Island (Arctic Ocean)	212 200/81 910
(20) Ireland (Atlantic Ocean)	83 045/32 055

Longest/shortest Coastlines

Longest		*Shortest*	
Canada	152 110 miles	Monaco	3.5 miles
Russia	64 000 miles	Nauru	12 miles
Indonesia	25 000 miles	Bosnia	13 miles
Australia	22 826 miles	Jordan	16 miles
Japan	20 684 miles	Slovenia	19 miles
Norway	13 264 miles	Zaire	24 miles
USA	12 380 miles	Iraq	28 miles
China	11 500 miles	Togo	31 miles

The above include offshore islands and some (e.g. China) are
estimated but reasonably accurate.

Land-locked Countries
(excluding coasts on lakes e.g. the Caspian Sea)

Africa
Botswana, Burkina Faso, Burundi, Central African Republic, Chad, Ethiopia, Lesotho, Malawi, Mali, Niger, Rwanda, Swaziland, Uganda, Zambia, Zimbabwe

Asia
Afghanistan, Armenia, Azerbaijan, Bhutan, Kazakhstan, Kyrgyzstan, Laos, Mongolia, Nepal, Tajikistan, Turkmenistan, Uzbekistan

Europe
Andorra, Austria, Belarus, Czech Republic, Hungary, Liechtenstein, Luxembourg, Macedonia, Moldova, San Marino, Slovakia, Switzerland, the Vatican City

South America
Bolivia, Paraguay

Largest Cities

Country	Metropolitan Area (City)	Population
Mexico	Mexico City	18 748 000
Brazil	Sao Paulo	17 113 000
USA	New York	16 198 000
Egypt	Cairo	15 000 000
China	Shanghai	13 342 000
Argentina	Buenos Aires	12 604 000
India	Bombay	12 572 000
Japan	Tokyo	11 936 000

Brazil	Rio de Janeiro	11 206 000
South Korea	Seoul	10 979 000
India	Calcutta	10 916 000
USA	Los Angeles	10 845 000
China	Beijing (formerly Peking)	10 819 000
Indonesia	Jakarta	9 253 000
France	Paris	9 060 000
Russia	Moscow	9 000 000
China	Tianjin (Tientsin)	8 785 000
United Kingdom	London	8 620 000
Japan	Osaka	8 520 000
India	Delhi	8 375 000

Countries, Capitals and Currencies

Country	Capital City	Currency
Afghanistan	Kabul	afghani
Albania	Tirana	lek
Algeria	Algiers	dinar
Andorra	Andorra La Vella	franc or peso
Angola	Luanda	kwanza
Antigua & Barbuda	St John's	east caribbean dollar
Argentina	Buenos Aires	peso
Armenia	Yerevan	dram
Australia	Canberra	dollar
Austria	Vienna	schilling
Azerbaijan	Baku	manat
Bahamas	Nassau	dollar
Bahrain	Manama	dinar
Bangladesh	Dhaka	taka
Barbados	Bridgetown	dollar
Belarus	Minsk	rouble

Belgium	Brussels	franc
Belize	Belmopan	dollar
Benin	Porto Novo	franc
Bhutan	Thimphu	ngultrum
Bolivia	La Paz	boliviano
Bosnia–Herzegovina	Sarajevo	dinar
Botswana	Gaborone	pula
Brazil	Brasília	cruzeiro
Brunei	Bandar Seri Begawan	dollar
Bulgaria	Sofia	lev
Burkina Faso	Ouagadougou	franc
Burundi	Bujumbura	franc
Cambodia	Phnom Penh	riel
Cameroon	Yaoundé	franc
Canada	Ottawa	dollar
Cape Verde	Praia	escudo
Central African Rep.	Bangui	franc
Chad	N'Djamena	franc
Chile	Santiago	peso
China	Beijing	yuan
Colombia	Bogotá	peso
Comoros	Moroni	franc
Congo	Brazzaville	franc
Costa Rica	San José	colón
Croatia	Zagreb	dinar
Cuba	Havana	peso
Cyprus	Nicosia	pound
Czech Republic	Prague	koruna
Denmark	Copenhagen	krone
Djibouti	Djibouti	franc
Dominica	Roseau	dollar

Dominican Republic	Santo Domingo	peso
Ecuador	Quito	sucre
Egypt	Cairo	pound
El Salvador	San Salvador	colón
Equatorial Guinea	Malabo	franc
Eritrea	Asmara	birr
Estonia	Tallinn	kroon
Ethiopia	Addis Ababa	birr
Fiji	Suva	dollar
Finland	Helsinki	markka
France	Paris	franc
Gabon	Libreville	franc
Gambia	Banjul	dalisi
Georgia	Tbilisi	rouble
Germany	Berlin	deutschmarc
Ghana	Accra	cedi
Greece	Athens	drachma
Grenada	St George's	dollar
Guatemala	Guatemala City	quetzel
Guinea	Conakry	franc
Guinea Bissau	Bissau	peso
Guyana	Georgetown	dollar
Haiti	Port-au-Prince	gourde
Honduras	Tegucigalpa	lempira
Hungary	Budapest	forint
Iceland	Reykjavík	króna
India	New Delhi	rupee
Indonesia	Jakarta	rupiah
Iran	Tehran	rial
Iraq	Baghdad	dinar
Ireland	Dublin	pound

Israel	Jerusalem	sheqel
Italy	Rome	lira
Jamaica	Kingston	dollar
Japan	Tokyo	yen
Jordan	Amman	dinar
Kazakhstan	Alma-Ata	tan'ga
Kenya	Nairobi	shilling
Kiribati	Bairiki	dollar
Korea, North	Pyongyang	won
Korea, South	Seoul	won
Kuwait	Kuwait	dinar
Kyrgyzstan	Bishkek	rouble
Laos	Vientiane	new kip
Latvia	Riga	rouble
Lebanon	Beirut	pound
Lesotho	Maseru	loti
Liberia	Monrovia	dollar
Libya	Tripoli	dinar
Liechtenstein	Vaduz	franc
Lithuania	Vilnius	rouble
Luxembourg	Luxembourg	franc
Macedonia	Skopje	dinar
Madagascar	Antananarivo	franc
Malawi	Lilongwe	kwacha
Malaysia	Kuala Lumpur	ringgit (dollar)
Maldives	Malé	rufiyaa
Mali	Bamako	franc
Malta	Valletta	lira
Marshall Islands	Majuro	dollar
Mauritania	Nouakchott	ouguiya
Mauritius	Port Louis	rupee

Mexico	Mexico City	peso
Micronesia	Kolonia	dollar
Moldova	Kishinev	rouble
Monaco	Monaco City	franc
Mongolia	Ulan Bator	tugrik
Morocco	Rabat	dirham
Mozambique	Maputo	metical
Myanmar (Burma)	Rangoon	kyat
Namibia	Windhoek	rand
Nauru	de facto capital Yaren	dollar
Nepal	Kathmandu	rupee
Netherlands	Amsterdam	guilder
	The Hague (seat of gov.)	
New Zealand	Wellington	dollar
Nicaragua	Managua	córdoba
Niger	Niamey	franc
Nigeria	Lagos	naira
	Abuja (seat of gov.)	
Norway	Oslo	krone
Oman	Muscat	rial
Pakistan	Islamabad	rupee
Panama	Panama City	balboa
Papua New Guinea	Port Moresby	kina
Paraguay	Asunción	guarani
Peru	Lima	inti
Philippines	Manila	peso
Poland	Warsaw	zloty
Portugal	Lisbon	escudo
Qatar	Doha	riyal
Romania	Bucharest	leu
Russia	Moscow	rouble

Rwanda	Kigali	franc
St Christopher & Nevis	Basseterre	dollar
(Also called St Kitts)		
St Lucia	Castries	dollar
St Vincent & the Grenadines	Kingstown	dollar
San Marino	San Marino	lira
Sao Tomé & Príncipe	Sao Tomé	dobra
Saudi Arabia	Riyadh	riyal
Senegal	Dakar	franc
Seychelles	Victoria	rupee
Sierra Leone	Freetown	leone
Singapore	Singapore	dollar
Slovakia	Bratislava	koruna
Slovenia	Ljubljana	tolar
Solomon Islands	Honiara	dollar
Somalia	Mogadishu	shilling
South Africa	Pretoria	rand
Spain	Madrid	peseta
Sri Lanka	Colombo	rupee
Sudan	Khartoum	pound
Suriname	Paramaribo	guilder
Swaziland	Mbabane	lilangeni
Sweden	Stockholm	krona
Switzerland	Berne	franc
Syria	Damascus	pound
Taiwan	Taipei	dollar
Tajikistan	Dushanbe	rouble
Tanzania	Dodoma (Legislative)	shilling
	Dar es Salaam (Admin.)	
Togo	Lomé	franc
Tonga	Nuku'alofa	pa'anga

Trinidad & Tobago	Port of Spain	dollar
Tunisia	Tunis	dinar
Turkey	Ankara	lira
Turkmenistan	Ashkabad	manat
Tuvalu	Funafuti	dollar
Uganda	Kampala	shilling
Ukraine	Kiev	hryvnia
United Arab Emirates	Abu Dhabi	dirham
United Kingdom	London	pound
U.S.A.	Washington, D.C.	dollar
Uruguay	Montevideo	peso
Uzbekistan	Tashkent	soum
Vanuatu	Port-Vila	vatu
Vatican City State	Vatican City	lira
Venezuela	Caracas	bolívar
Vietnam	Hanoi	dong
Western Samoa	Apia	tala
Yemen	San'a	riyal
Yugoslavia	Belgrade	new dinar
(Serbia & Montenegro)		
Zaïre	Kinshasa	zaïre
Zambia	Lusaka	kwacha
Zimbabwe	Harare	dollar

Countries which have changed name

Presently	Formerly
Belarus	Belorussia
Belize	British Honduras
Benin	Dahomey
Botswana	Bechuanaland
Burkina Faso	Upper Volta
Burundi	Urundi

Cambodia	Kampuchea
Central African Republic	Ubanghi Shari
East Timor	Portuguese Timor
Equatorial Guinea	Spanish Guinea
Ghana	Gold Coast
Guinea-Bissau	Portuguese Guinea
Guyana	British Guiana
Indonesia	Dutch East Indies
Iran	Persia
Jordan	Transjordan
Kiribati	Gilbert Islands
Kyrgyzstan	Khirgizia
Lesotho	Basutoland
Malawi	Nyasaland
Mali	French Sudan
Micronesia	Caroline Islands
Moldova	Moldavia
Myanmar	Burma
Namibia	S.W. Africa
Oman	Muscat & Oman
Sri Lanka	Ceylon
Surinam	Dutch Guiana
Tanzania	Tanganyika
Thailand	Siam
Tuvalu	Ellice Islands
United Arab Emirates	Trucial States
Vanuatu	New Hebrides
Western Sahara	Spanish Sahara
Zaïre	Belgian Congo
Zambia	N. Rhodesia
Zimbabwe	S. Rhodesia

Major World Airports (in volume of passengers)

1	O'Hare International	Chicago USA
2	Dallas	Fort Worth USA
3	Hartsfield International	Atlanta USA
4	Los Angeles International	California USA
5	Heathrow	London
6	Tokyo International	Japan
7	San Francisco International	California USA
8	John F. Kennedy International	New York USA
9	Frankfurt International	Germany
10	Stapleton International	Denver USA
11	Miami International	Florida USA
12	Orly	Paris

The United States of America

State	Nicknames	Admission	State Capital
Alabama	Heart of Dixie	22nd	Montgomery
	Cotton State		
	Yellowhammer State		
Alaska	The Last Frontier	49th	Juneau
	Land of the Midnight Sun		
Arizona	Grand Canyon State	48th	Phoenix
	Apache State		
Arkansas	Land of Opportunity	25th	Little Rock
	Wonder State		
	Bear State		
California	Golden State	31st	Sacramento
Colorado	Centennial State	38th	Denver
Connecticut	Constitution State	5th	Hartford
	Nutmeg State		
Delaware	First State	1st	Dover
	Diamond State		

Florida	Sunshine State	27th	Tallahassee
	Peninsula State		
Georgia	Empire State of the South	4th	Atlanta
	Peach State		
Hawaii	Aloha State	50th	Honolulu
Idaho	Gem State	43rd	Boise
	Gem of the Mountains		
Illinois	Prairie State	21st	Springfield
Indiana	Hoosier State	19th	Indianapolis
Iowa	Hawkeye State	29th	Des Moines
Kansas	Sunflower State	34th	Topeka
	Jayhawk State		
Kentucky	Bluegrass State	15th	Frankfort
Louisiana	Pelican State	18th	Baton Rouge
	Creole State		
	Sugar State		
	Bayou State		
Maine	Pine Tree State	23rd	Augusta
Maryland	Old Line State	7th	Annapolis
	Free State		
Massachusetts	Bay State	6th	Boston
	Old Colony State		
Michigan	Wolverine State	26th	Lansing
Minnesota	North Star State	32nd	St Paul
	Gopher State		
Mississippi	Magnolia State	20th	Jackson
Missouri	Show Me State	24th	Jefferson City
Montana	Treasure State	41st	Helena
Nebraska	Cornhusker State	37th	Lincoln
	Beef State		
	Tree Planters' State		

State	Nickname(s)		Capital
Nevada	Sagebrush State	36th	Carson City
	Silver State		
	Battle Born State		
New Hampshire	Granite State	9th	Concord
New Jersey	Garden State	3rd	Trenton
New Mexico	Land of Enchantment	47th	Sante Fe
	Sunshine State		
New York	Empire State	11th	Albany
North Carolina	Tar Heel State	12th	Raleigh
	Old North State		
North Dakota	Sioux State	39th	Bismarck
	Flickertail State		
Ohio	Buckeye State	17th	Columbus
Oklahoma	Sooner State	46th	Oklahoma City
Oregon	Beaver State	33rd	Salem
Pennsylvania	Keystone State	2nd	Harrisburg
Rhode Island	Little Rhody	13th	Providence
South Carolina	Palmetto State	8th	Columbia
South Dakota	Coyote State	40th	Pierre
	Sunshine State		
Tennessee	Volunteer State	6th	Nashville
Texas	Lone Star State	28th	Austin
Utah	Beehive State	45th	Salt Lake City
Vermont	Green Mountain State	14th	Montpelier
Virginia	The Old Dominion	10th	Richmond
	Cavalier State		
Washington	Evergreen State	42nd	Olympia
	Chinook State		
West Virginia	Mountain State	35th	Charleston
	Panhandle State		
Wisconsin	Badger State	30th	Madison
Wyoming	Equality State	44th	Cheyenne

International Vehicle Registration Letters

• •

A	Austria	D	Germany
AFG	Afghanistan	DK	Denmark
AL	Albania	DOM	Dominican Republic
AND	Andorra	DY	Benin
AUS	Australia	DZ	Algeria
B	Belgium	E	Spain
BD	Bangladesh	EAK	Kenya
BDS	Barbados	EAT	Tanzania
BER*	Belarus	EAU	Uganda
BG	Bulgaria	EAZ	Zanzibar (Tanzania)
BH	Belize	EC	Ecuador
BR	Brazil	ES	El Salvador
BRN	Bahrain	ET	Egypt
BRU	Brunei	ETH	Ethiopia
BS	Bahamas	EW*	Estonia
BUR	Burma (Myanmar)	F	France and territories
C	Cuba	FJI	Fiji
CDN	Canada	FL	Liechtenstein
CH	Switzerland	FR	Faeroe Islands
CI	Cote d'Ivoire (Ivory Coast)	GB	United Kingdom
		GBA	Alderney
CL	Sri Lanka	GBG	Guernsey
CO	Colombia	GBJ	Jersey
CR	Costa Rica	GBM	Isle of Man
CRO*	Croatia	GBZ	Gibraltar
CS	Czech Republic	GCA	Guatemala
CY	Cyprus	GH	Ghana

GR	Greece	MW	Malawi
GRU*	Georgia	N	Norway
GUY	Guyana	NA	Netherlands Antilles
H	Hungary	NIC	Nicaragua
HK	Hong Kong	NL	Netherlands
HKJ	Jordan	NZ	New Zealand
I	Italy	P	Portugal
IL	Israel	PA	Panama
IND	India	PAK	Pakistan
IR	Iran	PE	Peru
IRL	Ireland	PL	Poland
IRQ	Iraq	PNG	Papua New Guinea
IS	Iceland	PY	Paraguay
J	Japan	RA	Argentina
JA	Jamaica	RB	Botswana
K	Cambodia	RC	Taiwan
KWT	Kuwait	RCA	Central African
L	Luxembourg		Republic
LAO	Laos	RCB	Congo
LAR	Libya	RCH	Chile
LB	Liberia	RH	Haiti
LR*	Latvia	RI	Indonesia
LS	Lesotho	RIM	Mauritania
LT	Lithuania	RL	Lebanon
M	Malta	RM	Madagascar
MA	Morocco	RMM	Mali
MAL	Malaysia	RN	Niger
MC	Monaco	RO*	Russia
MEX	Mexico	RO	Romania
MOL*	Moldova	ROK	Korea
MS	Mauritius	ROU	Uruguay

RP	Philippines	UKR*	Ukraine
RSM	San Marino	USA	United States
RU	Burundi		of America
RWA	Rwanda	V	Vatican City
S	Sweden	VN	Vietnam
SD	Swaziland	WAG	Gambia
SF	Finland	WAL	Sierra Leone
SGP	Singapore	WAN	Nigeria
SLO*	Slovenia	WD	Dominica
SME	Suriname	WG	Grenada
SN	Senegal	WL	St Lucia
SQ*	Slovakia	WS	Western Samoa
SWA	Namibia	WV	St Vincent and
SY	Seychelles		the Grenadines
SYR	Syria	YU	Yugoslavia
T	Thailand	YV	Venezuela
TG	Togo	Z	Zambia
TN	Tunisia	ZA	South Africa
TR	Turkey	ZRE	Zaire
TT	Trinidad and Tobago	ZW	Zimbabwe

* indicates a registration that is in use but has not been officially accepted. Other countries either do not have registration letters or use letters that are not internationally recognised.

Literature

The years listed below refer to the year of award, not to the year of publication.

◆ ◆

Booker McConnell Prize Winners

1970	Bernice Rubens, *The Elected Member*
1971	V.S. Naipaul, *In a Free State*
1972	John Berger, G
1973	J.G. Farrell, *The Siege of Krishnapur*
1974	(Joint prize winners)
	Nadine Gordimer, *The Conservationist*
	Stanley Middleton, *Holiday*
1975	Ruth Prawer Jhabvala, *Heat and Dust*
1976	David Storey, *Saville*
1977	Paul Scott, *Staying On*
1978	Iris Murdoch, *The Sea, The Sea*
1979	Penelope Fitzgerald, *Offshore*
1980	William Golding, *Rites of Passage*
1981	Salman Rushdie, *Midnight's Children*
1982	Thomas Keneally, *Schindler's Ark*
1983	J.M. Coetzee, *Life & Times of Michael K*
1984	Anita Brookner, *Hotel du Lac*
1985	Keri Hulme, *The Bone People*
1986	Kingsley Amis, *The Old Devils*
1987	Penelope Lively, *Moon Tiger*
1988	Peter Carey, *Oscar and Lucinda*
1989	Kazuo Ishiguro, *The Remains of the Day*
1990	A.S. Byatt, *Possession*
1991	Ben Okri, *The Famished Road*

1992   (Joint prize winners)
        Michael Ondaatje, *The English Patient*
        Barry Unsworth, *Sacred Hunger*
1993   Roddy Doyle, *Paddy Clarke Ha Ha Ha*

Pulitzer Prize Winners (Fiction)

1950   A.B. Guthrie Jr., *The Way West*
1951   Conrad Richter, *The Town*
1952   Herman Wouk, *The Caine Mutiny*
1953   Ernest Hemingway, *The Old Man and the Sea*
1954   No Award
1955   William Faulkner, *A Fable*
1956   MacKinley Kantor, *Andersonville*
1957   No Award
1958   James Agee, *A Death in the Family*
1959   Robert Lewis Taylor, *The Travels of Jamie McPheeters*
1960   Allen Drury, *Advise and Consent*
1961   Harper Lee, *To Kill a Mockingbird*
1962   Edwin O'Conner, *The Edge of Sadness*
1963   William Faulkner, *The Reivers*
1964   No Award
1965   Shirely Ann Grau, *The Keepers of the House*
1966   Katherine Anne Porter,
        The Collected Stories of Katherine Anne Porter
1967   Bernard Malamud, *The Fixer*
1968   William Styron, *The Confessions of Nat Turner*
1969   N. Scott Momaday, *House Made of Dawn*
1970   Jean Stafford, *Collected Stories*
1971   No Award
1972   Wallace Stegner, *Angle of Repose*
1973   Eudora Welty, *The Optimist's Daughter*

1974	No Award
1975	Michael Shaara, *The Killer Angels*
1976	Saul Bellow, *Humboldt's Gift*
1977	No Award
1978	James Alan McPherson, *Elbow Room*
1979	John Cheever, *The Stories of John Cheever*
1980	Norman Mailer, *The Executioner's Song*
1981	John Kennedy Toole, *A Confederacy of Dunces*
1982	John Updike, *Rabbit is Rich*
1983	Alice Walker, *The Color Purple*
1984	William Kennedy, *Ironweed*
1985	Alison Lurie, *Foreign Affairs*
1986	Larry McMurtry, *Lonesome Dove*
1987	Peter Taylor, *A Summons to Memphis*
1988	Toni Morrison, *Beloved*
1989	Anne Tyler, *Breathing Lessons*
1990	Oscar Hijuelos, *The Mambo Kings Play Songs of Love*
1991	John Updike, *Rabbit at Rest*
1992	Jane Smiley, *A Thousand Acres*
1993	Robert Olen Butler, *A Good Scent from a Strange Mountain*

Nobel Prize Winners (Literature)

1950	Bertrand Russell (UK)
1951	Pär Lagerkvist (Sweden)
1952	François Mauriac (France)
1953	Sir Winston Churchill (UK)
1954	Ernest Hemingway (USA)
1955	Halldór Kiljan Laxness (Iceland)
1956	Juan Ramon Jiménez (Spain)
1957	Albert Camus (France)
1958	Boris Pasternak (USSR – prize declined)

1959	Salvatore Quasimodo (Italy)
1960	Saint-Jean Perse (France)
1961	Ivo Andríc (Yugoslavia)
1962	John Steinback USA)
1963	Giorgos Seferis (Greece)
1964	Jean-Paul Sartre (France)
1965	Mikhail Sholokhov (USSR)
1966	Samuel Joseph Agnon (Israel)/Nelly Sachs (West Germany)
1967	Miguel Angel Asturias (Guatamala)
1968	Yasunari Kawabata (Japan)
1969	Samuel Beckett (Ireland)
1970	Aleksandr I. Solzhenitsyn (USSR)
1971	Pablo Neruda (Chile)
1972	Heinrich Böll (West Germany)
1973	Patrick White (Australia)
1974	Eyvind Johnson/Harry Martinson (Sweden)
1975	Eugenio Montale (Italy)
1976	Saul Bellow (USA)
1977	Vicente Aleixandre (Spain)
1978	Isaac Bashevis Singer (USA)
1979	Odysseus Elytis (Greece)
1980	Czeslaw Milosz (Poland/USA)
1981	Elias Canetti (UK)
1982	Gabriel García Marquez (Colombia)
1983	William Golding (UK)
1984	Jaroslav Seifert (Czechoslovakia)
1985	Claude Simon (France)
1986	Wole Soyinka (Nigeria)
1987	Joseph Brodsky (USSR)
1988	Naguib Mahfouz (Egypt)
1989	Camilo José Cela (Spain)

1990   Octavio Paz (Mexico)
1991   Nadine Gordimer (South Africa)
1992   Derek Walcott (St Lucia)
1993   Toni Morrison (USA)

Plays of William Shakespeare

Titus Andronicus	*Published after his death*
Henry VI Part 2	Othello
The Taming of the Shrew	Henry IV Part 1
Henry VI Part 3	The Two Gentlemen of Verona
Romeo and Juliet	The Comedy of Errors
Richard II	King John
Richard III	As You Like It
Henry VI Part 1	Julius Caesar
Love's Labour's Lost	Twelfth Night
Henry IV Part 2	Measure for Measure
A Midsummer Night's Dream	All's Well That Ends Well
The Merchant of Venice	Macbeth
Much Ado About Nothing	Timon of Athens
Henry V	Antony and Cleopatra
Sir John Falstaff and the Merry	Coriolanus
Wives of Windsor	Cymbeline
Hamlet	The Winter's Tale
King Lear	The Tempest
Pericles, Prince of Tyre	Henry VIII
Troilus and Cressida	

Well-known Noms de Plume

Acton Bell	Anne Brontë
Currer Bell	Charlotte Brontë
Ellis Bell	Emily Brontë
Nicholas Blake	Cecil Day Lewis

Boz	Charles Dickens
Lewis Carroll	Charles Lutwidge Dodgson
Elia	Charles Lamb
George Eliot	Mary Ann Evans
Maxim Gorky	Aleksei Peshkov
O. Henry	William Sydney Porter
John Le Carré	David Cornwell
George Orwell	Eric Arthur Blair
Ellery Queen	Used by the co-authors Frederic Dannay and his cousin Manfred B. Lee
Saki	Hector Hugh Munro
George Sand	Amandine Aurore Lucie Dupin, Baronne Dudevant
Stendhal	Marie-Henri Beyle
Mark Twain	Samuel Langhorne Clemens
Voltaire	François-Marie Arouet
Mary Westmacott	Agatha Christie

Nursery Rhymes

Nursery rhymes provide another fertile source for all quiz masters.
Listed below are some of the more popular ones.

Monday's child is fair of face,
Tuesday's child is full of grace,
Wednesday's child is full of woe,
Thursday's child has far to go,
Friday's child is loving and giving,
Saturday's child works hard for a living,
And the child that was born on the Sabbath day is bonny and blithe,
and good and gay.

Solomon Grundy,
Born on a Monday,
Christened on Tuesday,
Married on Wednesday,
Took ill on Thursday,
Worse on Friday,
Died on Saturday,
Buried on Sunday,
This is the end
Of Solomon Grundy.

As I was going to St Ives,
I met a man with seven wives,
Each wife had seven sacks,
Each sack had seven cats,
Each cat had seven kits:
Kits, cats, sacks, and wives,
How many were there going to St Ives?

If the question is put 'How many wives, sacks, cats and kittens were going to St Ives?', then the answer is none. If, however, the question is phrased 'How many were going to St Ives?', then the answer is one.

Ten little Indians went out to dine;
One choked his little self, and then there were nine.

Nine little Indians sat up very late;
One overslept himself, and then there were eight.

Eight little Indians travelling in Devon;
One said he'd stay there, and then there were seven.

Seven little Indians chopping up sticks;
One chopped himself in half, and then there were six.

Six little Indians playing with a hive;
A bumble-bee stung one, and then there were five.

Five little Indians going in for law;
One got in Chancery, and then there were four.

Four little Indians going out to sea;
A red herring swallowed one, and then there were three.

Three little Indians walking in the Zoo;
A big bear hugged one, and then there were two.

Two little Indians sitting in the sun;
One got frizzled up, and then there was one.

One little Indian living all alone;
He got married, and then there were none.

Oranges and Lemons,
Say the bells of St Clement's.

You owe me five farthings,
Say the bells of St Martins'.

When will you pay me?
Say the bells of Old Bailey.

When I grow rich,
Say the bells of Shoreditch.

When will that be?
Say the bells of Stepney.

I'm sure I don't know,
Say the great bell at Bow.

Here comes a candle to light you to bed,
Here comes a chopper to chop off your head.

Odds and Sods

This section is dedicated to all the questions which are presented time and time again but which don't fit easily in to any other category.

◆ ◆

12

Twelve Signs of the Zodiac:

Aries	The Ram	21 March–19 April
Taurus	The Bull	20 April–20 May
Gemini	The Twins	21 May–21 June
Cancer	The Crab	22 June–22 July
Leo	The Lion	23 July–22 August
Virgo	The Virgin	23 August–22 September
Libra	The Scales	23 September–21 October
Scorpio	The Scorpion	24 October–21 November
Sagittarius	The Archer	22 November–21 December
Capricorn	The Goat	22 December–19 January
Aquarius	The Water Carrier	20 January–18 February
Pisces	The Fishes	19 February–20 March

Twelve Apostles:

(according to Matthew, Mark, Luke and the Acts)

Peter

Andrew (brother of Peter)

James, son of Zebedee

John (brother of James)

Philip

Bartholomew (also known as Nathaniel)

Thomas (the doubter)

Matthew

James, son of Alphaeus

Simon the Caanite (also known as Simon Zelotes)
Thaddeus or Jude (also referred to as Judas—not Iscariot)
Judas Iscariot

Twelve Gods of Olympus	(Roman equivalent)
Zeus, Lord of all the Olympian Gods, God of the Sky and all therein	(Jupiter)
Hera, wife of Zeus, Goddess of the Sky, of Women and Marriage	(Juno)
Poseidon, God of the Sea and Earthquakes	(Neptune)
Demeter, Goddess of the Harvest	(Ceres)
Apollo, God of Music	
Artemis, Goddess of the Young, Chastity and Childbirth	(Diana)
Ares, God of War	(Mars)
Aphrodite, Goddess of Beauty and Love	(Venus)
Hermes, God of Travellers and Trade	(Mercury)
Athene, Goddess of Wise Council and Prudence	(Minerva)
Hephaestus, God of Metalcraft and Fire	(Vulcan)
Hestia, Goddess of Fire	(Vesta)

Twelve Months of the Year—associated birthstones and flowers:

January	Garnet	Carnation/snowdrop
February	Amethyst	Violet/primrose
March	Aquamarine/bloodstone	Jonquil/violet
April	Diamond	Daisy/sweet pea
May	Emerald	Hawthorn/lily of the valley
June	Pearl/alexandrite/moonstone	Rose/honeysuckle
July	Ruby	Larkspur/water lily
August	Peridot/sardonyx	Gladiolus/poppy
September	Sapphire	Morning glory/aster
October	Opal/tourmaline	Calendula/cosmos
November	Topaz	Chrysanthemum
December	Turquoise/zircon	Narcissus/holly/poinsettia

8

Eight American states beginning with the letter M:
Maine, Maryland, Minnesota, Mississippi, Missouri, Montana, Massachusetts, Michigan

Eight reindeers of Santa:
Dasher, Dancer, Donner, Blitzen, Comet, Cupid, Prancer, Vixen

Eight horses on which Lester Piggott won the St Leger:
St Paddy, Aurelius, Ribocco, Ribero, Nijinsky, Athens Wood, Boucher, Commanche Run

7

Seven Wonders of the World:
Pyramids of Giza (Egypt), Tomb of Mausolus, King of Caria, Temple of Diana/Artemis at Ephesus, Walls and Hanging Gardens of Babylon, Colossus of Rhodes, Ivory and Gold Statue of Jupiter/Zeus at Olympia, The Pharos or WatchTower at Alexandria

Seven heraldic colours:
Azur (Blue), Gules (Red), Purpure (Purple), Sable (Black), Vert (Green), Argent (Silver), Or (Gold)

Seven dwarfs:
Dopey, Sneezy, Doc, Sleepy, Grumpy, Happy, Bashful

Seven cardinal virtues:
Justice, Prudence, Temperance, Fortitude, Faith, Hope, Charity

Seven deadly sins:
Pride, Covetousness, Lust, Anger, Gluttony, Envy, Sloth

The Magnificent Seven (survivors in brackets):
(Yul Brynner, Steve McQueen, Horst Bucholst), Brad Dexter, Robert Vaughn, Charles Bronson, Charles Coburn

Seven Manchester United post-war managers:
Matt Busby, Wilf McGuinness, Frank O'Farrell, Tommy Docherty, Dave Sexton, Ron Atkinson, Alex Ferguson

Seven players who were in Liverpool's first two European Cup winning teams 1977/78:
Ray Clemence, Phil Neal, Ray Kennedy, Emlyn Hughes, Jimmy Case, Steve Heighway, Terry McDermott

6

Six countries into which the Alps extend:
Italy, France, Switzerland, Austria, Germany, Liechtenstein
Six players who have been elected European Footballer of the Year more than once:
Alfredo Di Stefano, Johann Cruyff, Franz Beckenbauer, Kevin Keegan, Karl-Heinz Rummenigge, Michel Platini
Six original tokens used in *Monopoly*:
Top hat, motor car, ship, boot, flat iron, dog
Six characters in *Cluedo*:
Mrs White, Reverend Green, Miss Scarlett, Colonel Mustard, Professor Plum, Mrs Peacock
Six Bond films which starred Sean Connery:
GoldFinger, Doctor No, From Russia with Love, Thunder Ball, You Only Live Twice, Diamonds Are Forever, Never Say Never Again
Six male members of the Tracy family in Thunderbirds:
Scott, Virgil, Alan, Gordon, John, Jef

5

Five continents:
Europe, Africa, Asia, America, Australasia
Five Bond films of the 70s:
Diamonds Are Forever, Live and Let Die, The Man with the Golden Gun, The Spy Who Loved Me, Moonraker
Five Vincent O'Brien derby winners:
Nijinsky, Roberto, Sir Ivor, Larkspur, The Minstrel

Five English flat race classics in order:
1000 Guineas, 2000 Guineas, the Derby, the Oaks, the St Leger
Five boxers who beat Muhammed Ali:
Joe Frazier, Ken Norton, Leon Spinks, Larry Holmes, Trevor Berbick
Five Marx brothers:
Groucho, Chico, Harpo, Zeppo, Gummo

4

Four American states beginning with NEW:
New Hampshire, New Mexico, New Jersey, New York
Four quarter-days:
Midsummer, Christmas, Lady, Michaelmas
Four Goons:
Spike Milligan, Harry Secombe, Peter Sellers, Michael Bentine
Four vultures from the Jungle Book:
John, Paul, George, Ringo
Four great Shakespearean tragedies:
Hamlet, Macbeth, Othello, King Lear
Four British boxers who challenged Muhammed Ali in world
championship contests:
Henry Cooper, Joe Bugner, Brian London, Richard Dunn

3

Three sons of Adam and Eve:
Cain, Abel, Seth
Three angels mentioned by name in the Bible:
Gabriel, Michael, Lucifer
Three boxers who beat Joe Louis:
Max Schmelling, Ezzard Charles, Rocky Marciano
Three West Ham players in England's 1966 World Cup
winning team:
Bobby Moore, Geoff Hurst, Martin Peters

Three Magi/Wise Men:

Melchior, Caspar, Balthazar

2

Two surnames of Bonny and Clyde:

Parker and Barrow

Two players who won the women's doubles at Wimbledon five
times between 1967–1973:

Billie Jean King and Rosie Casals

Two racing classics held at Newmarket:

1000 and 2000 Guineas

Two heavyweights who fought for the vacant title when Rocky
Marciano retired:

Floyd Patterson and Archie Moore

Two captains in the 1966 World Cup Final:

Bobby Moore and Uwe Seeler

1

One tie for best actress Oscar:

Barbra Streisand and Katharine Hepburn

One witch mentioned by name in the Bible:

The witch of Endor

One American President who was a bachelor:

James Buchanan

One American President impeached:

Andrew Johnson

One F.A. Cup medal winner in consecutive years for
different teams:

Brian Talbot (Ipswich and Arsenal)

Wedding Anniversaries

1st	Cotton	13th	Lace
2nd	Paper	14th	Ivory
3rd	Leather	15th	Crystal
4th	Fruit and Flowers	20th	Porcelain
5th	Wood	25th	Silver
6th	Sugar	30th	Pearl
7th	Wool/Copper	35th	Coral
8th	Bronze/Pottery	40th	Ruby
9th	Pottery/Willow	45th	Sapphire
10th	Tin	50th	Golden
11th	Steel	60th	Diamond
12th	Silk/Linen	70th	Platinum

Patron Saints

◆ ◆

Patron Saints for Professions

Accountants	St Matthew
Actors	St Genesius
	St Vitus
Advertisers	St Bernardino of Siena
Altar Boys	St John Berchmans
Archers	St Sebastian
Architects	St Thomas the Apostle
	St Benedict the Abbot
	St Barbara
Artists	St Luke
Astronomers	St Dominic
Athletes	St Sebastian
Authors	St Francis de Sales

Aviators	Our Lady of Loreto
	St Joseph of Cupertino
Bakers	St Honoratus
	St Elizabeth of Hungary
Bankers	St Michael the Archangel
	St Matthew
	St Bernardino of Feltre
Barbers	St Cosmas
	St Damian
Blacksmiths	St Eligius (Eloi)
	St Dunstan
Bookkeepers	St Matthew
Booksellers	St John of God
Brewers	St Amand
	St Wenceslaus
Bricklayers	St Stephen
	St Thomas the Apostle
Builders	St Vincent Ferrer
Butchers	St Luke
	St Adrian of Nicomedia
Carpenters	St Anne
	St Joseph
Comedians	St Vitus
Cooks	St Lawrence
	St Martha
Dairy Workers	St Brigid
Dentists	St Apollonia
Doctors	St Luke
	St Damian
	St Cosmas
	St Pantaleon

Editors	St John Bosco
	St Francis de Sales
Engineers	St Barbara
	St Ferdinand III
	St Benedict
Farmers	St Isidore the Farmer
	St Benedict the Abbot
Firemen	St Agatha
	St Laurence
Fishermen	St Peter, Prince of the Apostles
	St Andrew the Apostle
Florists	St Dorothy
	St Rose of Lima
	St Thérèse of Lisieux
Gardeners	St Fiacre
	St Phocas
	St Rose of Lima
Glassworkers	St Lucy
Grave-diggers	St Joseph of Arimethea
Grocers	St Michael
Housewives	St Martha
	St Zita
Hunters	St Hubert
	St Eustace
Infantrymen	St Maurice
	St Martin de Tours
Innkeepers	St Gentian
	St Amand
Jewellers	St Eligius (Eloi)
Journalists	St Francis de Sales
Jurists	St John of Capistrano

Labourers	St Joseph
	St Isidore (farm workers)
	St John Bosco (young workers)
Lawyers	St Raymund
	St Hilary
	St Ivo
	St Thomas More
Librarians	St Jerome
	St Catherine of Alexandria
Maids	St Zita
Merchants	St Francis of Assisi
	St Homobonus
	St Nicholas of Bari
Metalworkers	St Eligius (Eloi)
Miners	St Anne
	St Barbara
Mountaineers	St Bernard of Montjoux
Musicians	St Cecilia
	St Gregory the Great
Nurses	St Camillus de Lellis
	St John of God
Orators	St John Chrysostom
Painters	St Luke
	St Fra Angelico
Paratroopers	St Michael the Archangel
Pawnbrokers	St Bernardino of Feltre
	St Nicholas of Bari
Pharmacists	St Cosmas
	St Damian
Philosophers	St Justin
	St Catherine of Alexandria

Policemen	St Michael the Archangel
Postal Workers	St Gabriel the Archangel
Priests	St Jean-Baptiste Vianney
Printers	St John of God
	St Augustine of Hippo
Sailors	St Nicholas of Bari
	St Christopher
	St Francis of Paola
	St Erasmus
Scholars	St Jerome
	St Thomas Aquinas
Scientists	St Albert the Great
Sculptors	St Luke
Secretaries	St Mark
	St Genesius
Servants	St Martha
	St Zita
Shoemakers	St Crispin
	St Crispinian
Singers	St Gregory the Great
	St Cecilia
Skaters	St Lidwina
Skiers	St Bernard
	BV Mary Our Lady of Graces
Social Workers	St Louise de Marillac
	St John Francis Regis
Soldiers	St Martin of Tours
	St Maurice
	St George
	St Sebastian
	St Joan of Arc

Students	St Thomas Aquinas
	St Catherine of Alexandria
Tailors	St Homobonus
Tax Collectors	St Matthew
Taxi Drivers	St Fiacre
Teachers	St John Baptist de la Salle
Theologians	St John the Apostle
	St Augustine
	St Thomas Aquinas
	St Alphonsus Liguori
Travellers	St Christopher
	St Nicholas of Bari
	St Joseph
	St Raphael the Archangel
Undertakers	St Dismas
	St Joseph of Arimathea
Writers	St John the Apostle
	St Francis de Sales

National Patron Saints

Country	Saint	Date
Argentina	BV Mary Our Lady of Lujan	–
Austria	St Leopold	15 November
	St Florian	4 May
Belgium	St Joseph	19 March
Brazil	BV Mary Immaculate Aparecida	11 May
Bulgaria	St Cyril and St Methodius	7 July/14 February
Canada	St Joseph	19 March
	St Anne	26 July
Central America	St James the Great	25 July
	BV Mary Our Lady of Guadalupe	12 December

Chile	BV Mary Our Lady of Mount Carmel 16 July	
Colombia	BV Mary Our Lady of Chiquinquira 18 November	
Croatia	BV Mary Feast of the Assumption 15 August	
	St Nicholas Tavelic	14 November
	St Leopold Mandic	30 July
Cyprus	St Barnabus the Apostle	11 June
Czech Republic	St Wenceslaus	28 September
	St Ludmila	16 September
Denmark	St Anskar	3 February
England	St George	23 April
Finland	St Henry of Finland	19 January
France	St Joan of Arc	30 May
	BV Mary Feast of the Assumption 15 August	
	St Denis, Bishop of Paris	9 October
Germany	St Boniface	5 June
Holland	St Willibrord	7 November
Hungary	St Stephen of Hungary	16 August
	BV Mary Great Queen of Hungary 8 October	
Iceland	St Anskar	3 February
	St Thorlac	23 December
India	St Francis Xavier	3 December
	BV Mary Patron of India	–
Ireland	St Patrick	17 March
	St Brigid	1 February
Italy	St Catherine of Siena	29 April
	St Francis of Assisi	4 October
Jordan	St John the Baptist	29 August
Liechtenstein	BV Mary Feast of the Assumption 15 August	
Lithuania	St Casimir of Poland	4 March
	St Cunegund	3 March

Luxembourg	St Willibrord	7 November
	St Cunegund	3 March
Madagascar	St Vincent de Paul	27 September
Malta	St Paul the Apostle	29 June
Mexico	BV Mary Our Lady of Guadalupe	12 December
Moldova	St Cyril and St Methodius	7 July
Nigeria	St Patrick	17 March
	BV Mary Queen of Nigeria	–
North Africa	St Augustine	28 August
	St Cyprian	16 September
Norway	St Olaf	29 July
Pakistan	St Francis Xavier	3 December
	St Thomas the Apostle	3 July
Peru	St Rose of Lima	23 August
	St Joseph	19 March
Philippines	BV Mary Immaculate	11 February
	St Pudentiana	19 May
	St Rose of Lima	23 August
Poland	St Casimir of Poland	4 March
	St Stanislaus Kostka	13 November
	St Florian	4 May
Portugal	St Anthony of Padua	13 June
	BV Mary Immaculate	11 February
	St Francis Borgia	10 October
Romania	St Cyril and St Methodius	7 July/14 February
Russia	St Nicholas of Bari	6 December
	St Joseph	19 March
	St Andrew the Apostle	30 November
San Marino	St Marinus	4 September
Scotland	St Andrew the Apostle	30 November
	St Margaret of Scotland	16 November

Serbia	St Sava	14 January
Slovakia	St Cyril and St Methodius	7 July/14 February
South America	St Faith	6 October
Spain	St James the Greater	25 July
	BV Mary Immaculate Conception	8 December
	St Ferdinand	30 May
Sweden	St Bridget of Sweden (Birgitta)	23 July
	St Eric	18 May
Switzerland	St Nicholas von Flue	25 September
Turkey	St John the Apostle	27 December
	St George	23 April
Ukraine	St Vladimir	15 July
USA	BV Mary Immaculate Conception	8 December
Uruguay	BV Mary Our Lady of the 33	–
	St Philip and St James	3 May
Venezuela	BV Mary Our Lady of Coromoto	11 September
Vietnam	St Joseph	19 March
Wales	St David	1 March

Phobias

◆ ◆

Achluophobia	Darkness or night
Acrophobia	Heights
Agoraphobia	Open spaces
Ailurophobia	Cats
Altophobia	Heights
Androphobia	Men
Anthophobia	Flowers
Apiphobia	Bees
Arachnophobia	Spiders
Astraphobia	Lightning

Automysophobia	Being dirty
Bathophobia	Falling from a high place
Brontophobia	Thunder
Carnophobia	Meat
Cheimatophobia	Cold
Chromatophobia	Colour
Claustrophobia	Enclosed spaces
Cryophobia	Ice or frost
Cynophobia	Dogs
Dendrophobia	Trees
Electrophobia	Electricity
Entomophobia	Insects
Ergophobia	Work
Gallophobia	France or things French
Genophobia	Sex
Genuphobia	Knees
Germanophobia	Germany or things German
Gymnophobia	Nudity
Gynophobia	Women
Haematophobia	Blood
Heliophobia	Sunlight
Hippophobia	Horses
Hydrophobia	Water
Hypnophobia	Sleep
Hypsophobia	High places (falling from)
Ichthyophobia	Fish
Kinetophobia	Motion
Kleptophobia	Stealing
Linophobia	String
Musophobia	Mice
Mysophobia	Dirt or contamination

Necrophobia	Dead bodies or death
Nelophobia	Glass
Ochlophobia	Crowds
Ommatophobia	Eyes
Ophidiophobia	Snakes
Ornithophobia	Birds
Paedophobia	Children
Pantophobia	Everything
Phagophobia	Eating
Phasmophobia	Ghosts
Phyllophobia	Leaves
Pogonophobia	Beards
Potophobia	Alcoholic drink
Pteronophobia	Feathers
Russophobia	Russia or things Russian
Sciophobia	Shadows
Sinophobia	China or things Chinese
Tachophobia	Speed
Thalassophobia	Sea
Theophobia	God
Topophobia	Places
Triskaidekaphobia	Number 13
Xenophobia	Foreigners or things foreign

Politics

◆ ◆

Presidents of Ireland

1	Dr Douglas Hyde	1938–45
2	Sean Thomas O'Kelly	1945–59
3	Eamon de Valera	1959–73
4	Erskine Childers	1973–4

5	Cearbhall O'Dalaigh	1974–6
6	Dr Patrick Hillery	1976–90
7	Mary Robinson	1990–

Taoisigh of Ireland
(known as President of the Executive Council 1922–1937)

1	William Thomas Cosgrave	1922–32
2	Eamon de Valera	1932–48
3	John A. Costello	1948–51
4	Eamon de Valera	1951–4
5	John A. Costello	1954–7
6	Eamon de Valera	1957–9
7	Sean Lemass	1959–66
8	John Mary (Jack) Lynch	1966–73
9	Liam Cosgrave	1973–7
10	John Mary (Jack) Lynch	1977–9
11	Charles Haughey	1979–81
12	Garret FitzGerald	1981–2
13	Charles Haughey	1982
14	Garret FitzGerald	1982–7
15	Charles Haughey	1987–92
16	Albert Reynolds	1992–

Presidents of the United States of America

1	George Washington (Federalist)	1789–97
2	John Adams (Federalist)	1797–1801
3	Thomas Jefferson (Democratic Republican)	1801–9
4	James Madison (Democratic Republican)	1809–17
5	James Monroe (Democratic Republican)	1817–25
6	John Quincy Adams (Democratic Republican)	1825–9
7	Andrew Jackson (Democrat)	1829–37
8	Martin Van Buren (Democrat)	1837–41

9	William Henry Harrison (Whig)	1841
10	John Tyler (Whig)	1841–5
11	James K. Polk (Democrat)	1845–9
12	Zachary Taylor (Whig)	1849–50
13	Millard Fillmore (Whig)	1850–3
14	Franklin Pierce (Democrat)	1853–7
15	James Buchanan (Democrat)	1857–61
16	Abraham Lincoln (Republican)	1861–5
		(assassinated)
17	Andrew Johnson (Democrat)	1865–9
18	Ulysses Simpson Grant (Republican)	1869–77
19	Rutherford Birchard Hayes (Republican)	1877–81
20	James Abram Garfield (Republican)	1881
		(assassinated)
21	Chester Alan Arthur (Republican)	1881–5
22	Grover Cleveland (Democrat)	1885–9
23	Benjamin Harrison (Republican)	1889–93
24	Grover Cleveland (Democrat)	1893–7
25	William McKinley (Republican)	1897–1901
		(assassinated)
26	Theodore Roosevelt (Republican)	1901–9
27	William Howard Taft (Republican)	1909–13
28	Woodrow Wilson (Democrat)	1913–21
29	Warren Gamaliel Harding (Republican)	1921–3
30	Calvin Coolidge (Republican)	1923–9
31	Herbert Clark Hoover (Republican)	1929–33
32	Franklin Delano Roosevelt (Democrat)	1933–45
33	Harry S. Truman (Democrat)	1945–53
34	Dwight David Eisenhower (Republican)	1953–61
35	John Fitzgerald Kennedy (Democrat)	1961–3
		(assassinated)

36	Lyndon Baines Johnson (Democrat)	1963–9
37	Richard Milhous Nixon (Republican)	1969–74 (resigned)
38	Gerald Rudolph Ford (Republican)	1974–7
39	James Earl Carter (Democrat)	1977–81
40	Ronald Wilson Reagan (Republican)	1981–9
41	George Bush (Republican)	1989–93
42	William J. Clinton (Democrat)	1993–

British Prime Ministers since 1900

Marquess of Salisbury (Conservative)	1895–1902
Arthur James Balfour (Conservative)	1902–5
Sir Henry Campbell–Bannerman (Liberal)	1905–8
Herbert Henry Asquith (Liberal)	1908–16
David Lloyd George (Liberal)	1916–22
Andrew Bonar Law (Conservative)	1922–3
Stanley Baldwin (Conservative)	1923, 1924–9, 1935–7
James Ramsay Macdonald (Labour)	1924, 1929–35
Arthur Neville Chamberlain (Conservative)	1937–40
Sir Winston Churchill (Conservative)	1940–5, 1951–5
Clement Attlee (Labour)	1945–51
Sir Anthony Eden (Conservative)	1955–7
Harold Macmillan (Conservative)	1957–63
Sir Alexander Douglas–Home (Conservative)	1963–4
Harold Wilson (Labour)	1964–70, 1974–6
Edward Heath (Conservative)	1970–4
James Callaghan (Labour)	1976–9
Margaret Thatcher (Conservative)	1979–90
John Major (Conservative)	1990–

Women who are or have been
Head of State[†]/Head of Government[*]

Sirimavo Bandaranaike*	Sri Lanka (1960–65, 1970–77)
Indira Gandhi*	India (1966–77, 1980–84)
Golda Meir*	Israel (1969–74)
Isabelita Peron[†]	Argentina (1974–6)
Soong Ching–ling[†]	China (1976–8)
Margaret Thatcher*	UK (1979–90)
Maria de Lourdes Pintassilago*	Portugal (1979–80)
Lidia Gueiler Tejada[†]	Bolivia (1979–80)
Vigdis Finnbogadottir[†]	Iceland (1980–)
Eugenia Charles*	Dominica (1980–)
Gro Harlem Bruntland*	Norway (1981, 1986–9, 1990–)
Agatha Barbara[†]	Malta (1982–7)
Milka Planinc*	Yugoslavia (1982–6)
Corazon Aquino[†]	The Philippines (1986–92)
Benazir Bhutto*	Pakistan (1988–90, 1993–)
Violetta Chamorro[†]	Nicaragua (1990–)
Ertha Pascal–Trouillot[†]	Haiti (1990–91)
Mary Robinson[†]	Ireland (1990–)
Edith Cresson*	France (1991–2)
Khalida Zia*	Bangladesh (1991–)
Hannah Suchocka*	Poland (1992–)

Notable Political Assassinations this Century

William McKinley	USA (1901)
King Carlos I	Portugal (1908)
Archduke Franz Ferdinand	Austria (1914)
Leon Trotsky	Russia (1940)
Mohandas (Mahatma) Gandhi	India (1948)
King Faisal II	Iraq (1958)

John F. Kennedy	USA (1963)
H.F. Verwoerd	South Africa (1966)
Martin Luther King Jr.	USA (1968)
Robert Kennedy	USA (1968)
King Faisal	Saudi Arabia (1975)
Anwar Sadat	Egypt (1981)
Indira Gandhi	India (1984)
Olof Palme	Sweden (1986)
Rajiv Gandhi	India (1991)

The United Nations

There are six main divisions within the United Nations:

The Secretariat

The General Assembly

The Security Council

The Economic and Social Council

The Trusteeship Council

The International Court of Justice

All the above divisions are based in New York except The International Court of Justice which sits in The Hague.

Secretary-Generals of the United Nations

Trygve Lie	Norway (1946–53)
Dag Hammarskjöld	Sweden (1953–61)
U Thant	Burma (1961–71)
Kurt Waldheim	Austria (1972–81)
Javier Pérez de Cuéllar	Peru (1982–91)
Boutros Boutros-Ghali	Egypt (1992–)

The European Union

Members of the EU and their year of joining:

| Belgium | 1950 |
| Denmark | 1973 |

France	1950
Germany	1950
Greece	1981
Ireland	1973
Italy	1950
Luxembourg	1950
The Netherlands	1950
Portugal	1986
Spain	1986
United Kingdom	1973

The European Parliament is made up of 567 members (MEPs) and meets in Strasbourg. The committees meet in Brussels and The Secretariat in Luxembourg.

Breakdown of MEPs:

Germany	99
France	87
Italy	87
United Kingdom	87
Spain	64
The Netherlands	31
Belgium	25
Greece	25
Portugal	25
Denmark	16
Ireland	15
Luxembourg	6

Nobel Foundation

The Nobel Foundation is named after its benefactor Alfred Nobel, a Swedish chemist and industrialist whose fortune was made through his invention of dynamite. The Foundation endows six prizes annually, five of which are awarded by the relevent Swedish academies and institutions. These are: Chemistry, Literature, Physiology or Medicine, Physics and Economic Sciences. The sixth, the Nobel Peace Prize, is awarded by the Norwegian Nobel Committee.

Nobel Peace Prize Winners since 1960

1960	Albert Luthuli (South Africa)
1961	Dag Hammarskjöld (Sweden)
1962	Linus Pauling (USA)
1963	International Red Cross Committee
1964	Martin Luther King Jr. (USA)
1965	United Nations Children's Fund (UNICEF)
1966–67	No Award
1968	Rene Cassin (France)
1969	International Labour Organisation
1970	Norman Borlaug (USA)
1971	Willy Brandt (Germany)
1972	No Award
1973	Henry Kissinger (USA)
	Le Duc Tho (N. Vietnam — award declined)
1974	Eisaku Sato (Japan)
	Sean MacBride (Ireland)
1975	Andrei Sakharov (USSR)
1976	Mairead Corrigan (N. Ireland)
	Betty Williams (N. Ireland)
1977	Amnesty International
1978	Menachem Begin (Israel)
	Anwar Sadat (Egypt)

1979	Mother Teresa (India)
1980	Adolfo Esquivel (Argentina)
1981	United Nations High Commission for Refugees
1982	Alva Myrdal (Sweden)
	Alfonso Robles (Mexico)
1983	Lech Walesa (Poland)
1984	Archbishop Desmond Tutu (South Africa)
1985	International Physicians for the Prevention of Nuclear War
1986	Elie Wiesel (Romania-USA)
1987	Oscar Sanchez (Costa Rica)
1988	United Nations Peacekeeping Forces
1989	Dalai Lama (Tibet (exiled spirital leader))
1990	Mikhail Gorbachev (USSR)
1991	Aung San Suu Kyi (Myanmar)
1992	Rigoberta Menchú (Guatemala)
1993	Nelson Mandela (South Africa)
	F. W. de Klerk (South Africa)

Princes and Monarchs

◆ ◆

The House of York

Edward IV	1461–70
	1471–83
Edward V	1483
Richard III	1483–5

The House of Tudor

Henry VII	1485–1509
Henry VIII	1509–47
Edward VI	1547–53
Mary I	1553–8
Elizabeth I	1558–1603

The House of Stuart
James I   1603–25
Charles I   1625–49

Commonwealth Council of State   1649–53
Oliver Cromwell Lord Protector   1653–8
Richard Cromwell Lord Protector 1658–9

The Stuart Restoration
Charles II   1660–85
James II   1685–8

The House of Orange
William III and Mary II   1689–94
William III   1689–1702

The House of Stuart
Anne   1702–14

The House of Hanover
George I   1714–27
George II   1727–60
George III   1760–1820
George IV   1820–30
William IV   1830–7
Victoria   1837–1901

The House of Saxe-Coburg-Gotha
Edward VII   1901–10

The House of Windsor
George V   1910–36
Edward VIII   1936 (325 days)
George VI   1936–52
Elizabeth II   since 1952

Order of Succession to the Throne

1 HRH Prince Charles, Prince of Wales
2 HRH Prince William
3 HRH Prince Henry
4 HRH Prince Andrew, Duke of York
5 HRH Princess Beatrice
6 HRH Princess Eugenie
7 HRH Prince Edward
8 HRH Princess Anne, Princess Royal
9 Peter Phillips, son of Princess Anne
10 Zara Phillips, daughter of Princess Anne
11 HRH Princess Margaret
12 Viscount Linley, David Armstrong-Jones
13 Lady Sarah Armstrong-Jones

Quantities

◆ ◆

Numbers

Decimal to Binary

1	=	1	11	=	1011
2	=	10	12	=	1100
3	=	11	13	=	1101
4	=	100	14	=	1110
5	=	101	15	=	1111
6	=	110	16	=	10000
7	=	111	17	=	10001
8	=	1000	18	=	10010
9	=	1001	19	=	10011
10	=	1010	20	=	10100

Arabic to Roman

1	=	I	15	=	XV
2	=	II	20	=	XX
3	=	III	25	=	XXV
4	=	IV	30	=	XXX
5	=	V	40	=	XL
6	=	VI	50	=	L
7	=	VII	60	=	LX
8	=	VIII	70	=	LXX
9	=	IX	80	=	LXXX
10	=	X	90	=	XC
11	=	XI	100	=	C
12	=	XII	200	=	CC
13	=	XIII	500	=	D
14	=	XIV	1000	=	M

Measures

Fluid Capacity

8 fluid drahms	=	1 fluid ounce
5 fluid ounces	=	1 gill
4 gills	=	1 pint
2 pints	=	1 quart
4 quarts	=	1 gallon
2 gallons	=	1 peck
4 pecks	=	1 bushel
8 bushels	=	1 quarter
36 gallons	=	1 bulk barrel

Oil and Petroleum

34.97 UK gallons	=	1 barrel
42 US gallons	=	1 barrel
10 millilitres	=	1 centilitre

10 centilitres	=	1 decilitre
10 decilitres	=	1 litre
10 litres	=	1 decalitre
10 decalitres	=	1 hectolitre
10 hectolitres	=	1 kilolitre

Linear Measures

12 inches	=	1 foot
3 feet	=	1 yard
5½ yards	=	1 rod, pole or perch
4 rods	=	1 chain
10 chains	=	1 furlong
5280 feet	=	1 mile
1760 yards	=	1 mile
8 furlongs	=	1 mile

10 millimetres	=	1 centimetre
10 centimetres	=	1 decimetre
10 decimetres or 1000 millimetres	=	1 metre
10 metres	=	1 decametre
10 decametres	=	1 hectometre
10 hectometres or 1000 metres	=	1 kilometre

Metric Equivalents (to two decimal places)

1 centimetre	=	0.39 inches
1 inch	=	2.54 centimetres
1 metre	=	39.37 inches
1 yard	=	0.91 metres
1 kilometre	=	1093.6 yards
1 mile	=	1.61 kilometres
1 litre	=	1.76 pints
1 pint	=	0.57 litres
1 kilogram	=	2.2 lbs
1 pound	=	0.45 kilograms

Wines, Spirits and Beers

Wines and Spirits

tot	=	⅙ or ⅕ gill (In Ireland, ¼ gill)
noggin	=	1 gill
bottle	=	1⅓ pints

Champagne

2 bottles	=	1 magnum
4 bottles	=	1 jeroboam
20 bottles	=	nebuchadnezzar

Beer

nip	=	¼ pint
small	=	½ pint
large	=	1 pint
flagon	=	1 quart
anker	=	10 gallons
tun	=	216 gallons

Paper Sizes

Imperial

Large Post	=	16½" × 21" (419 × 533.4 mm)
Demy	=	17½" × 22½" (444.5 × 571.5 mm)
Medium	=	18" × 23" (457.2 × 584.2 mm)
Royal	=	20" × 25" (508 × 635 mm)
Double Crown	=	20" × 30" (508 × 762 mm)

'A' Series (metric)

A0	=	841 × 1189 mm
A1	=	594 × 841 mm
A2	=	420 × 594 mm
A3	=	297 × 420 mm
A4	=	210 × 297 mm
A5	=	148 × 210 mm

Science and Space

◆ ◆

Chemical Symbols (Periodic Table)

H	Hydrogen	Ni	Nickel
He	Helium	Cu	Copper
Li	Lithium	Zn	Zinc
Be	Beryllium	Ga	Gallium
B	Boron	Ge	Germanium
C	Carbon	As	Arsenic
N	Nitrogen	Se	Selenium
O	Oxygen	Br	Bromine
F	Fluorine	Kr	Krypton
Ne	Neon	Rb	Rubidium
Na	Sodium	Sr	Strontium
Mg	Magnesium	Y	Yttrium
Al	Aluminium	Zr	Zirconium
Si	Silicon	Nb	Niobium
P	Phosphorus	Mo	Molybdenum
S	Sulphur	Tc	Technetium
Cl	Chlorine	Ru	Ruthenium
Ar	Argon	Rh	Rhodium
K	Potassium	Pd	Palladium
Ca	Calcium	Ag	Silver
Sc	Scandium	Cd	Cadmium
Ti	Titanium	In	Indium
V	Vanadium	Sn	Tin
Cr	Chromium	Sb	Antimony
Mn	Manganese	Te	Tellurium
Fe	Iron	I	Iodine
Co	Cobolt	Xe	Xenon

Cs	Caesium	Bi	Bismuth
Ba	Barium	Po	Polonium
La	Lanthanum	At	Astatine
Ce	Cerium	Rn	Radon
Pr	Praseodymium	Fr	Francium
Nd	Neodymium	Ra	Radium
Pm	Promethium	Ac	Actinium
Sm	Samarium	Th	Thorium
Eu	Europium	Pa	Protactinium
Gd	Gadolinium	U	Uranium
Tb	Terbium	Np	Neptunium
Dy	Dysprosium	Pu	Plutonium
Ho	Holmium	Am	Americium
Er	Erbium	Cm	Curium
Tm	Thulium	Bk	Berkelium
Yb	Ytterbium	Cf	Californium
Lu	Lutetium	Es	Einsteinium
Hf	Hafnium	Fm	Fermium
Ta	Tantalum	Md	Mendelevium
W	Tungsten	No	Nobelium
Re	Rhenium	Lr	Lawrencium
Os	Osmium	Unq	Unnilquadium
Ir	Iridium	Unp	Unnilpentium
Pt	Platinum	Unh	Unnilhexium
Au	Gold	Uns	Unnilseptium
Hg	Mercury	Uno	Unniloctium
Tl	Thallium	Une	Unnilennium
Pb	Lead		

Inventions and Inventors

Aeroplane (with motor)	Wilbur and Orville Wright
Barbed Wire	Lucien Smith
Barometer	Evangelista Torricelli
Battery (electric)	Alessandro Volta
Bicycle Tyres (pneumatic)	John Boyd Dunlop
Bunsen Burner	Robert Bunsen
Carpet Sweeper	Melville Bissell
Cash Register	James Ritty
Chronometer	John Harrison
Electric Iron	H.W. Seeley
Electric Lamp (incandescent)	Thomas Alva Edison
Engine, diesel	Rudolf Diesel
Engine, jet	Frank Whittle
Engine, steam (condenser)	James Watt
Engine, steam (piston)	Thomas Newcomen
Fountain Pen	Lewis E. Waterman
Glider	Sir George Cayley
Gramaphone	Thomas Alva Edison
Hovercraft	Christopher Cockerell
Launderette	J.F. Cantrell
Lift (mechanical)	Elisha G. Otis
Lightning Conductor	Benjamin Franklin
Linoleum	Frederick Walton
Match (safety)	John Walker
Micro-processor	Marcian Hoff
Microscope	Zacharias Janssen
Motor Cycle	Gottlieb Daimler
Neon Lamp	Georges Claude
Nylon	Wallace Carothers
Parachute	Jean-Pierre Blanchard

Parking Meter	Carlton C. Magee
Radio Telegraphy	Guglielmo Marconi
Razor (electric)	Jacob Schick
Razor (safety)	King Gillette
Record (LP)	Peter Goldmark
Rubber (latex foam)	Dunlop Rubber Co.
Rubber (vulcanised)	Charles Goodyear
Safety Pin	Walter Hunt
Scotch Tape	Richard Drew
Slide Rule	William Oughtred
Spinning Frame	Richard Arkwright
Spinning Jenny	James Hargreaves
Spinning Mule	Samuel Crompton
Steel (stainless)	Harry Brearley
Steel Production Process	Henry Bessemer
Tank	Ernest Swinton
Telegraph Code (magnetic)	Samuel Morse
Telephone	Alexander Graham Bell
Telescope	Hans Lippershey
Thermometer	Galilei Galileo
Transformer	Michael Faraday
Welder (electric)	Elisha Thomson
X-Rays	Wilhelm Rontgen
Zip Fastener	Whitcomb L. Judson

Planets in the Solar System and their Satellites

Planet	Number	Satellite Names
Mercury	0	
Venus	0	
Earth	1	Moon
Mars	2	Phobos, Deimos

Jupiter	16	Adastrea, Amalthea, Ananke, Callisto, Carme, Elara, Europa, Ganymede, Himalia, Io, Leda, Lysithea, Metis, Pasiphae, Sinope, Thebe
Saturn	18	Atlas, Calypso, Dione, Enceladus, Epimetheus, Helene, Hyperion, Iapetus, Janus, Mimas, Pan, Pandora, Phoebe, Prometheus, Rhea, Telesto, Tethys, Titan
Uranus	15	Ariel, Belinda, Bianca, Cordelia, Cressida, Desdemona, Juliet, Miranda, Oberon, Ophelia, Portia, Puck, Rosalind, Titania, Umbriel
Neptune	8	Despina, Galatea, Larissa, Naiad, Nereid, Proteus, Thalassa, Triton
Pluto	1	Charon

Milestones in Manned Space Flight

12 April 1961	USSR: First manned space flight, Yuri Gagarin in Vostok 1.
5 May 1961	USA: First US-manned space flight 'Sub-orbital', Alan Shepard in *Liberty Bell 7*.
20 February 1962	USA: First US orbital space flight, John Glenn in *Friendship 7*.
11–15 August 1962	USSR: First simultaneous space flights, Andrian Nikolayev in *Vostok 3*, and Pavel Popovich in *Vostok 4*.
16–19 June 1963	USSR: First woman in space, Valentina Tereshkova in *Vostok 6*.
18 March 1965	USSR: First space walk, Alexei Leonov in *Voskhod 2*.
3–7 June 1965	USA: First US space walk, Edward White in *Gemini 4*.

16 December 1965	USA: First rendezvous in space, Walter Schirra Jr. and Thomas Stafford in *Gemini* 6 and *Gemini* 7.
27 January 1967	USA: Virgil Grissom, Edward White and Roger Chaffee died during a practice.
21–27 December 1968	USA: First manned flight round the moon, Frank Borman, James Lovell, William Anders in *Apollo* 8.
16 January 1969	USSR: First transfer of crew members from one spacecraft to another. Yevgeny Khrunov and Alexei Yeliseyev spacewalked from *Soyuz* 5 to *Soyuz* 4.
18 May 1969	USA: First to fly solo in lunar orbit, John Young.
20 July 1969	USA: First men to walk on the moon, Neil Armstrong followed by Buzz Aldrin, *Apollo* 11.
April 19 1971	USSR: First space station launched, *Salyut 1*. It was manned for 23 days by Georgi Dobrovolsky.
11 December 1972	USA: Last *Apollo* Moon mission touches down on the Moon with Eugene Cernan and Jack Schmitt in *Apollo* 17.
25 May 1973	USA: First US space station launched, *Skylab*. Last crew splashed down 8 February 1974.
16–18 July 1975	USSR/USA: First international space docking, *Soyuz* 19 and *Apollo* 18.
12–14 April 1981	USA: First flight of a reusable space vehicle. John Young and Robert Crippen in the space shuttle *Colombia*.
6 August 1981	USSR: Youngest person in space, Gherman Stepanovich, aged 25.

18 June 1983	USA: First US woman in space, Sally Ride in the space shuttle *Challenger*.
17 July 1984	USSR: First female space walker, Svetlana Savitskaya.
8 November 1984	USA: First mother in space, Anna Fisher in the space shuttle *Discovery*.
12 April 1985	USA: First passenger-observer in space, Jake Garn.
28 January 1986	USA: All seven crew (five men and two women) aboard the space shuttle *Challenger* died in a tragic explosion shortly after lift-off.
2 December 1990	USA: Oldest person in space, Vance Brand, aged 59.
18 May 1991	First Briton in space, Helen Sharman.

Sport

The following are lists of winners of major sporting events both at home and abroad. Unfortunately, at the time of going to press, we are unable to include all the 1994 winners! For this, no doubt, we have all bookmakers' everlasting gratitude.

◆ ◆

Horse Racing

Grand National

1994	Miinnehoma	R. Dunwoody
1993	Void*	
1992	Party Politics	C. Llewllyn
1991	Seagram	N. Hawke
1990	Mr Frisk	Mr M. Armytage
1989	Little Polveir	J. Frost

* This race was void due to a false start. Esha Ness ridden by John White finished first past the post.

1988	Rhyme 'n' Reason	B. Powell
1987	Maori Venture	S. Knight
1986	West Tip	R. Dunwoody
1985	Last Suspect	H. Davies
1984	Hallo Dandy	N. Doughty
1983	Corbiere	B. de Haan
1982	Grittar	Mr D. Saunders
1981	Aldaniti	B. Champion
1980	Ben Nevis	Mr C. Fenwick
1979	Rubstick	M. Barnes
1978	Lucius	B. Davies
1977	Red Rum	T. Stack
1976	Rag Trade	J. Burke
1975	L'Escargot	T. Carberry
1974	Red Rum	B. Fletcher
1973	Red Rum	B. Fletcher
1972	Well To Do	G. Thorner
1971	Specify	J. Cook
1970	Gay Trip	P. Taaffe

Cheltenham Gold Cup

1994	The Fellow	A. Kondrat
1993	Jodami	M. Dwyer
1992	Cool Ground	A. Maguire
1991	Garrison Savannah	M. Pitman
1990	Norton's Coin	G. McCourt
1989	Desert Orchid	S. Sherwood
1988	Charter Party	R. Dunwoody
1987	The Thinker	R. Lamb
1986	Dawn Run	J. J. O'Neill
1985	Forgive 'n' Forget	M. Dwyer

1984	Burrough Hill Lad	*P. Tuck*
1983	Bregawn	*G. Bradley*
1982	Silver Buck	*R. Earnshaw*
1981	Little Owl	*Mr A. J. Wilson*
1980	Master Snudge	*R. Hoare*
1979	Alverton	*J. J. O'Neill*
1978	Midnight Court	*J. Francome*
1977	Davy Lad	*D. Hughes*
1976	Royal Frolic	*J. Burke*
1975	Ten Up	*T. Carberry*
1974	Captain Christy	*B. Beasley*
1973	The Dikler	*R. Barry*
1972	Glencaraig Lady	*F. Berry*
1971	L'Escargot	*T. Carberry*
1970	L'Escargot	*T. Carberry*

Champion Hurdle

1994	Flakey Dove	*M. Dwyer*
1993	Granville Again	*P. Scudamore*
1992	Royal Gait	*G. McCourt*
1991	Morley Street	*J. Frost*
1990	Kribensis	*R. Dunwoody*
1989	Beech Road	*R. Guest*
1988	Celtic Shot	*P. Scudamore*
1987	See You Then	*S. Smith Eccles*
1986	See You Then	*S. Smith Eccles*
1985	See You Then	*S. Smith Eccles*
1984	Dawn Run	*J. J. O'Neill*
1983	Gaye Brief	*R. Linley*
1982	For Auction	*Mr C. Magnier*
1981	Sea Pigeon	*J. Francome*

1980	Sea Pigeon	J. J. O'Neill
1979	Monksfield	D. Hughes
1978	Monksfield	T. Kinane
1977	Night Nurse	P. Broderick
1976	Night Nurse	P. Broderick
1975	Comedy of Errors	K. White
1974	Lanzarote	R. Pitman
1973	Comedy of Errors	B. Smith
1972	Bula	P. Kelleway
1971	Bula	P. Kelleway
1970	Persian War	J. Uttley

1,000 Guineas

1994	Las Meninas	J. Reid
1993	Sayyedati	W. Swinburn
1992	Hatoof	W. Swinburn
1991	Shadayid	W. Carson
1990	Salsabil	W. Carson
1989	Musical Bliss	W. Swinburn
1988	Ravinella	G. Moore
1987	Miesque	F. Head
1986	Midway Lady	R. Cochrane
1985	Oh So Sharp	S. Cauben
1984	Pebbles	P. Robinson
1983	Ma Biche	F. Head
1982	On the House	J. Reid
1981	Fairy Footsteps	L. Piggott
1980	Quick as Lightning	B. Rouse
1979	One in a Million	J. Mercer
1978	Enstone Spark	E. Johnson
1977	Mrs McArdy	E. Hide

1976	Flying Water	Y. Saint-Martin
1975	Nocturnal Spree	J. Roe
1974	Highclere	J. Mercer
1973	Mysterious	G. Lewis
1972	Waterloo	E. Hide
1971	Altesse Royale	Y. Saint-Martin
1970	Humble Duty	L. Piggott

2,000 Guineas

1994	Mister Baileys	J. Weaver
1993	Zafonic	P. Eddery
1992	Rodrigo de Triano	L. Piggott
1991	Mystiko	M. Roberts
1990	Tirol	M. Kinane
1989	Nashwan	W. Carson
1988	Doyoun	W. Swinburn
1987	Don't Forget Me	W. Carson
1986	Dancing Brave	G. Starkey
1985	Shadeed	L. Piggott
1984	El Gran Senor	P. Eddery
1983	Lomond	P. Eddery
1982	Zino	F. Head
1981	To-Agori-Mou	G. Starkey
1980	Known Fact	W. Carson
1979	Tap On Wood	S. Cauthen
1978	Roland Gardens	F. Durr
1977	Nebbiolo	G. Curran
1976	Wollow	G. Dettori
1975	Bolkonski	G. Dettori
1974	Nonoalco	Y. Saint-Martin
1973	Mon Fils	F. Durr

1972	High Top	W. Carson
1971	Brigadier Gerard	J. Mercer
1970	Nijinsky	L. Piggott

The Derby

1994	Erhaab	W. Carson
1993	Commander in Chief	M. Kinane
1992	Dr Devious	J. Reid
1991	Generous	A. Munro
1990	Quest for Fame	P. Eddery
1989	Nashwan	W. Carson
1988	Kahyasi	R. Cochrane
1987	Reference Point	S. Cauthen
1986	Shahrastani	W. Swinburn
1985	Slip Anchor	S. Cauthen
1984	Secreto	C. Roche
1983	Teenoso	L. Piggott
1982	Golden Fleece	P. Eddery
1981	Shergar	W. Swinburn
1980	Henbit	W. Carson
1979	Troy	W. Carson
1978	Shirley Heights	G. Starkey
1977	The Minstrel	L. Piggott
1976	Emprey	L. Piggott
1975	Grundy	P. Eddery
1974	Snow Knight	B. Taylor
1973	Morston	E. Hide
1972	Roberto	L. Piggott
1971	Mill Reef	G. Lewis
1970	Nijinsky	L. Piggott

The Oaks

1994	Balanchine	F. Dettori
1993	Intrepidity	M. Roberts
1992	User Friendly	G. Duffield
1991	Jet Ski Lady	C. Roche
1990	Salsabil	W. Carson
1989*	Snow Bride	S. Cauthen
1988	Diminuendo	S. Cauthen
1987	Unite	W. Swinburn
1986	Midway Lady	R. Cochrane
1985	Oh So Sharp	S. Cauthen
1984	Circus Plume	L. Piggott
1983	Sun Princess	W. Carson
1982	Time Charter	B. Newnes
1981	Blue Wind	L. Piggott
1980	Bireme	W. Carson
1979	Scintillate	P. Eddery
1978	Fair Salinia	G. Starkey
1977	Dunfermline	W. Carson
1976	Pawneese	Y. Saint-Martin
1975	Juliette Marny	L. Piggott
1974	Polygamy	P. Eddery
1973	Mysterious	G. Lewis
1972	Ginevra	T. Murray
1971	Altesse Royale	G. Lewis
1970	Lupe	S. Barclay

* Aliysa finished first but was disqualified.

The St Leger

1993	Bob's Return	P. Robinson
1992	User Friendly	G. Duffield

1991	Toulon	P. Eddery
1990	Snurge	T. Quinn
1989	Michelozzo	S. Cauthen
1988	Minster Son	W. Carson
1987	Reference Point	S. Cauthen
1986	Moon Madness	P. Eddery
1985	Oh So Sharp	S. Cauthen
1984	Commanche Run	L. Piggott
1983	Sun Princess	W. Carson
1982	Touching Wood	P. Cook
1981	Cut Above	J. Mercer
1980	Light Cavalry	J. Mercer
1979	Son of Love	A. Laqueux
1978	Julio Mariner	E. Hide
1977	Dunfermline	W. Carson
1976	Crow	Y. Saint-Martin
1975	Bruni	T. Murray
1974	Bustino	J. Mercer
1973	Peleid	F. Durr
1972	Boucher	L. Piggott
1971	Athens Wood	L. Piggott
1970	Nijinsky	L. Piggott

King George VI and Queen Elizabeth Diamond Stakes

1993	Opera House	M. Roberts
1992	St Jovite	S. Craine
1991	Generous	A. Munro
1990	Belmez	M. Kinane
1989	Nashwan	W. Carson
1988	Mtoto	M. Roberts
1987	Reference Point	S. Cauthen

1986	Dancing Brave	P. Eddery
1985	Petoski	W. Carson
1984	Teenoso	L. Piggott
1983	Time Charter	J. Mercer
1982	Kalaglow	G. Starkey
1981	Shergar	W. Swinburn
1980	Ela-Mana-Mou	W. Carson
1979	Troy	W. Carson
1978	Ile de Bourbon	J. Reid
1977	The Minstrel	L. Piggott
1976	Pawnese	Y. Saint-Martin
1975	Grundy	P. Eddery
1974	Dahlia	L. Piggott
1973	Dahlia	W. Pyers
1972	Brigadier Gerard	J. Mercer
1971	Mill Reef	G. Lewis
1970	Nijinsky	L. Piggott

Irish Grand National

1994	Son of War	F. Woods
1993	Ebony Jane	C. Swan
1992	Vanton	J. Titley
1991	Omerta	A. Maguire
1990	Desert Orchid	R. Dunwoody
1989	Maid of Money	A. Powell
1988	Perris Valley	B. Sheridan
1987	Brittany Boy	T. Taaffe
1986	Insure	M. Flynn
1985	Rhyme 'n' Reason	G. Bradley
1984	Bentom Boy	Mrs A. Ferris
1983	Bit of a Skite	T. Ryan

1982	King Spruce	G. Newman
1981	Luska	T. V. Finn
1980	Daletta	J. P. Harty
1979	Tied Cottage	A. Robinson
1978	Brown Lad	G. Dowd
1977	Billycan	M. Morris
1976	Brown Lad	T. Carberry
1975	Brown Lad	T. Carberry
1974	Colebridge	E. Wright
1973	Tartan Ace	J. Cullen
1972	Dim Wit	M. Curran
1971	King's Sprite	A. Moore
1970	Garoupe	C. Finnegan

Irish Derby

1994	Balanchine	F. Dettori
1993	Commander in Chief	P. Eddery
1992	St Jovite	C. Roche
1991	Generous	A. Munro
1990	Salsabil	W. Carson
1989	Old Vic	S. Cauthen
1987	Sir Harry Lewis	J. Reid
1986	Shahrastani	W. Swinburn
1985	Law Society	P. Eddery
1984	El Gran Senor	P. Eddery
1983	Shareef Dancer	W. Swinburn
1982	Assert	C. Roche
1981	Shergar	L. Piggott
1980	Tyrnavos	T. Murray
1979	Troy	W. Carson
1978	Shirley Heights	G. Starkey

1977	The Minstrel	L. Piggott
1976	Malacate	P. Paquet
1975	Grundy	P. Eddery
1974	English Prince	Y. Saint-Martin
1973	Weavers Hall	G. McGrath
1972	Steel Pulse	B. Williamson
1971	Irish Ball	A. Gilbert
1970	Nijinsky	L. Ward

Irish 1,000 Guineas

1994	Mehthaff	W. Carson
1993	Nicer	M. Hills
1992	Marling	W. Swinburn
1991	Kooyonga	W. O'Connor
1990	In the Groove	S. Cauthen
1989	Ensconse	R. Cochrane
1988	Trusted Partner	M. Kinane
1987	Forest Flower	T. Ives
1986	Sonic Lady	W. Swinburn
1985	Al Bahathri	A. Murray
1984	Katies	P. Robinson
1983	L'Attrayante	A. Badel
1982	Princess Polly	W. Swinburn
1981	Arctique Royale	G. Curran
1980	Cairn Rouge	A. Murray
1979	Godetia	L. Piggott
1978	More So	C. Roche
1977	Lady Capulet	T. Murphy
1976	Sarah Siddons	C. Roche
1975	Miralla	R. Parnell
1974	Gaily	R. Hutchinson

1973	Cloonagh	G. Starkey
1972	Pidget	W. Swinburn
1971	Favoletta	L. Piggott
1970	Black Satin	R. Hutchinson

Irish 2,000 Guineas

1994	Turtle Island	J. Reid
1993	Barathea	M. Roberts
1992	Rodrigo de Triano	L. Piggott
1991	Fourstars Allstar	M. Smith
1990	Tirol	P. Eddery
1989	Shaadi	W. Swinburn
1988	Prince of Birds	D. Gillespie
1987	Don't Forget Me	W. Carson
1986	Flash of Steel	M. Kinane
1985	Triptych	C. Roche
1984	Sadler's Wells	G. McGrath
1983	Wassl	A. Murray
1982	Dara Monarch	M. Kinane
1981	King's Lake	P. Eddery
1980	Nikoli	C. Roche
1979	Dickens Hill	A. Murray
1978	Jaazeiro	L. Piggott
1977	Pampapaul	G. Dettori
1976	Northern Treasure	G. Curran
1975	Grundy	P. Eddery
1974	Furry Glen	G. McGrath
1973	Sharp Edge	J. Mercer
1972	Ballymore	C. Roche
1971	King's Company	F. Head
1970	Decies	L. Piggott

The Irish Oaks

1994	Bolas	P. Eddery
1993	Wemyss Bight	P. Eddery
1992	User Friendly	G. Duffield
1991	Possessive Dancer	S. Cauthen
1990	Knight's Baroness	T. Quinn
1989	Alydaress	M. Kinane
1988	Diminuendo	S. Cauthen } DEAD HEAT
	Melodist	W. Swinburn
1987	Unite	W. Swinburn
1986	Colorspin	P. Eddery
1985	Helen Street	W. Carson
1984	Princess Pati	P. Shanahan
1983	Give Thanks	D. Gillespie
1982	Swiftfoot	W. Carson
1981	Blue Wind	W. Swinburn
1980	Shoot a Line	W. Carson
1979	Godetia	L. Piggott
1978	Fair Salinia	G. Starkey
1977	Olwyn	J. Lynch
1976	Lagunette	P. Paquet
1975	Juliette Marny	L. Piggott
1974	Dibidale	W. Carson
1973	Dahlia	W. Pyers
1972	Regal Exception	M. Philipperon
1971	Altesse Royale	G. Lewis
1970	Santa Tina	L. Piggott

The Irish St Leger

1993	Vintage Crop	M. Kinane
1992	Maghaallah	S. Cauthen

1991	Turgeon	A. Cruz
1990	Ibn Bey	T. Quinn
1989	Petite Ile	R. Quinton
1988	Dark Lomond	D. Gillespie
1987	Eurobird	C. Asmussen
1986	Authaal	C. Roche
1985	Leading Counsel	P. Eddery
1984	Opale	D. McHargue
1983	Mountain Lodge	D. Gillespie
1982	Touching Wood	P. Cook
1981	Protection Racket	B. Taylor
1980	Gonzales	R. Carroll
1979	Niniski	W. Carson
1978	M-Lolshan	B. Taylor
1977	Transworld	T. Murphy
1976	Meneval	L. Piggott
1975	Caucasus	L. Piggott
1974	Mistigri	C. Roche
1973	Conor Pass	P. Jarman
1972	Pidget	T. Burns
1971	Parnell	A. Simpson
1970	Allangrange	G. McGrath

Prix de L'Arc de Triomphe

1993	Urban Sea	E. Saint-Martin
1992	Subotica	T. Jarnet
1991	Suave Dancer	C. Ashmussen
1990	Saumarez	G. Mosse
1989	Carroll House	M. Kinane
1988	Tony Bin	J. Reid
1987	Trempolino	P. Eddery

1986	Dancing Brave	*P. Eddery*
1985	Rainbow Quest	*P. Eddery*
1984	Sagace	*Y. Saint-Martin*
1983	All Along	*W. Swinburn*
1982	Akiyda	*Y. Saint-Martin*
1981	Gold River	*G. Moore*
1980	Detroit	*P. Eddery*
1979	Three Troikas	*F. Head*
1978	Alleged	*L. Piggott*
1977	Alleged	*L. Piggott*
1976	Ivanjica	*F. Head*

Greyhound Racing
English Derby

1994	Moral Standards	1986	Tico
1993	Ringa Hustle	1985	Pagan Swallow
1992	Farloe Melody	1984	Whisper Wishes
1991	Ballinderry Ash	1983	I'm Slippy
1990	Slippy Blue	1982	Laurie's Panther
1989	Lartigue Note	1981	Parkdown Jet
1988	Hit the Lid	1980	Indian Joe
1987	Signal Spark		

Irish Derby

1993	Daley's Dennis	1986	Kyle Jack
1992	Manx Treasure	1985	Tubbercurry Lad
1991	Ardfert Mick	1984	Dipmac
1990	The Other Toss	1983	Belvedere Bran
1989	Manorville Magic	1982	Cooladine Super
1988	Make History	1981	Bold Work
1987	Rathgallen Lady	1980	Suir Miller

Tennis

Wimbledon

Men's Singles

1994	Pete Sampras (USA)
1993	Pete Sampras (USA)
1992	Andre Agassi (USA)
1991	Michael Stich (Germany)
1990	Stefan Edberg (Sweden)
1989	Boris Becker (Germany)
1988	Stefen Edberg (Sweden)
1987	Pat Cash (Australia)
1986	Boris Becker (Germany)
1985	Boris Becker (Germany)
1984	John McEnroe (USA)
1983	John McEnroe (USA)
1982	Jimmy Connors (USA)
1981	John McEnroe (USA)
1980	Bjorn Borg (Sweden)
1979	Bjorn Borg (Sweden)
1978	Bjorn Borg (Sweden)
1977	Bjorn Borg (Sweden)
1976	Bjorn Borg (Sweden)
1975	Arthur Ashe (USA)
1974	Jimmy Connors (USA)
1973	Jan Kodes (Czechoslovakia)
1972	Stan Smith (USA)
1971	John Newcombe (Australia)
1970	John Newcombe (Australia)
1969	Rod Laver (Australia)
1968	Rod Laver (Australia)
1967	John Newcombe (Australia)

1966	Manuel Santana (Spain)
1965	Roy Emerson (Australia)
1964	Roy Emerson (Australia)
1963	Chuck McKinley (USA)
1962	Rod Laver (Australia)
1961	Rod Laver (Australia)
1960	Neale Fraser (Australia)
1959	Alex Olmedo (USA)
1958	Ashley Cooper (Australia)
1957	Lew Hoad (Australia)
1956	Lew Hoad (Australia)
1955	Tony Trabert (USA)
1954	Jaroslav Drobny (Czech)
1953	Vic Seixas (USA)
1952	Frank Sedgman (Australia)
1951	Dick Savitt (USA)
1950	Budge Patty (USA)
1949	Ted Schroeder (USA)
1948	Bob Falkenburg (USA)
1947	Jack Kramer (USA)
1946	Yvon Petra (France)

Women's Singles

1994	Conchita Martinez (Spain)
1993	Steffi Graf (Germany)
1992	Steffi Graf (Germany)
1991	Steffi Graf (Germany)
1990	Martina Navratilova (USA)
1989	Steffi Graf (Germany)
1988	Steffi Graf (Germany)
1987	Martina Navratilova (USA)

1986	Martina Navratilova (USA)
1985	Martina Navratilova (USA)
1984	Martina Navratilova (USA)
1983	Martina Navratilova (USA)
1982	Martina Navratilova (USA)
1981	Chris Evert-Lloyd (USA)
1980	Evonne Goolagong-Cawley (Aus)
1979	Martina Navratilova (USA)
1978	Martina Navratilova (USA)
1977	Virginia Wade (UK)
1976	Chris Evert (USA)
1975	Billie Jean King (USA)
1974	Chris Evert (USA)
1973	Billie Jean King (USA)
1972	Billie Jean King (USA)
1971	Evonne Goolagong (Australia)
1970	Margaret [Smith] Court (Australia)
1969	Ann Jones (UK)
1968	Billie Jean King (USA)
1967	Billie Jean King (USA)
1966	Billie Jean King née Moffitt (USA)
1965	Margaret Smith (Australia)
1964	Maria Bueno (Brazil)
1963	Margaret Smith (Australia)
1962	Karen Susman (USA)
1961	Angela Mortimer (UK)
1960	Maria Bueno (Brazil)
1959	Maria Bueno (Brazil)
1958	Althea Gibson (USA)
1957	Althea Gibson (USA)
1956	Shirley Fry (USA)

1955	Louise Brough (USA)
1954	Maureen Connolly (USA)
1953	Maureen Connolly (USA)
1952	Maureen Connolly (USA)
1951	Doris Hart (USA)
1950	Louise Brough (USA)
1949	Louise Brough (USA)
1948	Louise Brough (USA)
1947	Margaret Osborne (USA)
1946	Pauline Betz (USA)

Golf

US Open

Year	Winner	Year	Winner
1994	Ernie Els (S. Africa)	1977	Hubert Green
1993	Lee Janson	1976	Jerry Pate
1992	Tom Kite	1975	Lou Graham
1991	Payne Stewart	1974	Hale Irwin
1990	Hale Irwin	1973	Johnny Miller
1989	Curtis Strange	1972	Jack Nicklaus
1988	Curtis Strange	1971	Lee Trevino
1987	Scott Simpson	1970	Tony Jacklin (UK)
1986	Raymond Floyd	1969	Orville Moody
1985	Andy North	1968	Lee Trevino
1984	Fuzzy Zoeller	1967	Jack Nicklaus
1983	Larry Nelson	1966	Billy Casper
1982	Tom Watson	1965	Gary Player
1981	David Graham		(S. Africa)
	(Australia)	1964	Ken Venturi
1980	Jack Nicklaus	1963	Julius Boros
1979	Hale Irwin	1962	Jack Nicklaus
1978	Andy North	1961	Gene Littler

1960	Arnold Palmer	1952	Julius Boros
1959	Billy Casper	1951	Ben Hogan
1958	Tommy Bolt	1950	Ben Hogan
1957	Dick Mayer	1949	Cary Middlecoff
1956	Cary Middlecoff	1948	Ben Hogan
1955	Jack Fleck	1947	Lew Worsham
1954	Ed Furgol	1946	Lloyd Mangrum
1953	Ben Hogan		

British Open

1994	Nick Price (Zimbabwe)
1993	Greg Norman (Australia)
1992	Nick Faldo
1991	Ian Baker-Finch (Australia)
1990	Nick Faldo
1989	Mark Calcavecchia (USA)
1988	Severiano Ballesteros (Spain)
1987	Nick Faldo
1986	Greg Norman (Australia)
1985	Sandy Lyle
1984	Severiano Ballesteros (Spain)
1983	Tom Watson (USA)
1982	Tom Watson (USA)
1981	Bill Rogers (USA)
1980	Tom Watson (USA)
1979	Severiano Ballesteros (Spain)
1978	Jack Nicklaus (USA)
1977	Tom Watson (USA)
1976	Johnny Miller (USA)
1975	Tom Watson (USA)
1974	Gary Player (S. Africa)

1973	Tom Weiskopf (USA)
1972	Lee Trevino (USA)
1971	Lee Trevino (USA)
1970	Jack Nicklaus (USA)
1969	Tony Jacklin
1968.	Gary Player (S. Africa)
1967	Robert de Vicenzo (Argentina)
1966	Jack Nicklaus (USA)
1965	Peter Thomson (Australia)
1964	Tony Lema (USA)
1963	Bob Charles (New Zealand)
1962	Arnold Palmer (USA)
1961	Arnold Palmer (USA)
1960	Kel Nagle (Australia)
1959	Gary Player (S. Africa)
1958	Peter Thomson (Australia)
1957	Bobby Locke (S. Africa)
1956	Peter Thomson (Australia)
1955	Peter Thomson (Australia)
1954	Peter Thomson (Australia)
1953	Ben Hogan (USA)
1952	Bobby Locke (S. Africa)
1951	Max Faulkner
1950	Bobby Locke (S. Africa)
1949	Bobby Locke (S. Africa)
1948	Henry Cotton
1947	Fred Daly
1946	Sam Snead (USA)

US Masters

1994	Jose-Maria Olazabal (Spain)	1972	Jack Nicklaus
1993	Bernhard Langer (Germany)	1971	Charles Coody
1992	Fred Couples	1970	Billy Casper
1991	Ian Woosnam (UK)	1969	George Archer
1990	Nick Faldo (UK)	1968	Bob Goalby
1989	Nick Faldo (UK)	1967	Gay Brewer
1988	Sandy Lyle (UK)	1966	Jack Nicklaus
1987	Larry Mize	1965	Jack Nicklaus
1986	Jack Nicklaus	1964	Arnold Palmer
1985	Bernhard Langer (Germany)	1963	Jack Nicklaus
1984	Ben Crenshaw	1962	Arnold Palmer
1983	Severiano Ballesteros (Spain)	1961	Gary Player (S. Africa)
1982	Craig Stadler	1960	Arnold Palmer
1981	Tom Watson	1959	Art Wall, Jr.
1980	Severiano Ballesteros (Spain)	1958	Arnold Palmer
1979	Fuzzy Zoeller	1957	Doug Ford
1978	Gary Player (S. Africa)	1956	Jack Burke, Jr.
1977	Tom Watson	1955	Cary Middlecoff
1976	Raymond Floyd	1954	Sam Snead
1975	Jack Nicklaus	1953	Ben Hogan
1974	Gary Player (S. Africa)	1952	Sam Snead
1973	Tommy Aaron	1951	Ben Hogan
		1950	Jimmy Demaret
		1949	Sam Snead
		1948	Claude Harmon
		1947	Jimmy Demaret
		1946	Herman Keiser

US P.G.A.

1994	Nick Price (Zimbabwe)	1970	Dave Stockton
1993	Paul Azinger	1969	Ray Floyd
1992	Nick Price (Zimbabwe)	1968	Julius Boros
1991	John Daly	1967	Don January
1990	Wayne Grady (Australia)	1966	Al Geiberger
		1965	Dave Marr
1989	Payne Stewart	1964	Bobby Nichols
1988	Jeff Sluman	1963	Jack Nicklaus
1987	Larry Nelson	1962	Gary Player (S. Africa)
1986	Bob Tway		
1985	Hubert Green	1961	Jerry Barber
1984	Lee Trevino	1960	Jay Hebert
1983	Hal Sutton	1959	Rob Rosburg
1982	Ray Floyd	1958	Dow Finsterwald
1981	Larry Nelson	1957	Lionel Hebert
1980	Jack Nicklaus	1956	Jack Burke
1979	David Graham (Australia)	1955	Doug Ford
		1954	Chick Harbert
1978	John Mahaffey	1953	Walter Burkemo
1977	Lanny Watkins	1952	Jim Turnesa
1976	Dave Stockton	1951	Sam Snead
1975	Jack Nicklaus	1950	Chandler Harper
1974	Lee Trevino	1949	Sam Snead
1973	Jack Nicklaus	1948	Ben Hogan
1972	Gary Player (S. Africa)	1947	Jim Ferrier
		1946	Ben Hogan
1971	Jack Nicklaus		

Ryder Cup (USA v Europe)

	Winner	Course
1993	USA	The Belfry
1991	USA	Kiawah Island
1989	Tie	The Belfry
1987	Europe	Muirfield Village
1985	Europe	The Belfry
1983	USA	Palm Beach (PGA National)
1981	USA	Walton Heath
1979	USA	Greenbrier (Virginia)

World Matchplay Championship

1993	Corey Pavin beat Nick Faldo
1993	Corey Pavin beat Nick Faldo
1992	Nick Faldo beat Jeff Sluman
1991	Severiano Ballesteros beat Nick Price
1990	Ian Woosnam beat Mark McNulty
1989	Nick Faldo beat Ian Woosnam
1988	Sandy Lyle beat Nick Faldo
1987	Ian Woosnam beat Sandy Lyle
1986	Greg Norman beat Sandy Lyle
1985	Severiano Ballesteros beat Bernhard Langer
1984	Severiano Ballesteros beat Bernhard Langer
1983	Greg Norman beat Nick Faldo
1982	Severiano Ballesteros beat Sandy Lyle
1981	Severiano Ballesteros beat Ben Crenshaw
1980	Greg Norman beat Sandy Lyle
1979	Bill Rogers beat Isao Aoki
1978	Isoa Aoki beat Simon Owen
1977	Graham Marsh beat Ray Floyd

Soccer

League Cup Winners

1994	Aston Villa	1984	Liverpool
1993	Arsenal	1983	Liverpool
1992	Manchester United	1982	Liverpool
1991	Sheffield Wednesday	1981	Liverpool
1990	Nottingham Forest	1980	Wolves
1989	Nottingham Forest	1979	Nottingham Forest
1988	Luton	1978	Nottingham Forest
1987	Arsenal	1977	Aston Villa
1986	Oxford United	1976	Manchester City
1985	Norwich City	1975	Aston Villa

League Champions

1994	Manchester United	1984	Liverpool
1993	Manchester United	1983	Liverpool
1992	Leeds	1982	Liverpool
1991	Arsenal	1981	Aston Villa
1990	Liverpool	1980	Liverpool
1989	Arsenal	1979	Liverpool
1988	Liverpool	1978	Nottingham Forest
1987	Everton	1977	Liverpool
1986	Liverpool	1976	Liverpool
1985	Everton	1975	Derby

F. A. Cup Finals

1994	Manchester United 4, Chelsea 0
1993	Arsenal 1, Sheffield Wednesday 1
	Replay: Arsenal 2, Sheffield Wednesday 1
1992	Liverpool 2, Sunderland 0
1991	Tottenham 2, Nottingham Forest 1 (after extra time)

1990	Crystal Palace 3, Manchester United 3 (after extra time)
	Replay: Crystal Palace 0, Manchester United 1
1989	Liverpool 3, Everton 2 (after extra time)
1988	Wimbledon 1, Liverpool 0
1987	Coventry 3, Tottenham 2 (after extra time)
1986	Liverpool 3, Everton 1
1985	Manchester United 1, Everton 0
1984	Everton 2, Watford 0
1983	Manchester United 2, Brighton 2 (after extra time)
	Replay: Manchester United 4, Brighton 0
1982	Tottenham 1, Q.P.R. 1 (after extra time)
	Replay: Tottenham 1, Q.P.R. 0
1981	Tottenham 1, Manchester City 1 (after extra time)
	Replay: Tottenham 3, Manchester City 2
1980	West Ham 1, Arsenal 0
1979	Arsenal 3, Manchester United 2
1978	Ipswich 1, Arsenal 0
1977	Manchester United 2, Liverpool 1

Scottish F.A. Cup

1994	Dundee United	1984	Aberdeen
1993	Rangers	1983	Aberdeen
1992	Rangers	1982	Aberdeen
1991	Motherwell	1981	Rangers
1990	Aberdeen	1980	Celtic
1989	Celtic	1979	Rangers
1988	Celtic	1978	Rangers
1987	St Mirren	1977	Celtic
1986	Aberdeen	1976	Rangers
1985	Celtic	1975	Celtic

Scottish League Cup

1994	Rangers	1984	Rangers
1993	Rangers	1983	Celtic
1992	Hibernian	1982	Rangers
1991	Rangers	1981	Dundee United
1990	Aberdeen	1980	Dundee United
1989	Rangers	1979	Rangers
1988	Rangers	1978	Rangers
1987	Rangers	1977	Aberdeen
1986	Aberdeen	1976	Rangers
1985	Rangers	1975	Celtic

Scottish League Championship

1994	Rangers	1984	Aberdeen
1993	Rangers	1983	Dundee United
1992	Rangers	1982	Celtic
1991	Rangers	1981	Celtic
1990	Rangers	1980	Aberdeen
1989	Rangers	1979	Celtic
1988	Celtic	1978	Rangers
1987	Rangers	1977	Celtic
1986	Celtic	1976	Rangers
1985	Aberdeen	1975	Rangers

European Cup

1994	A. C. Milan	1988	P. S. V. Eindhoven
1993	Marseille	1987	F. C. Porto
1992	Barcelona	1986	Steaua Bucharest
1991	Red Star Belgrade	1985	Juventus
1990	A. C. Milan	1984	Liverpool
1989	A. C. Milan	1983	S. V. Hamburg

1982	Aston Villa	1978	Liverpool
1981	Liverpool	1977	Liverpool
1980	Nottingham Forest	1976	Bayern Munich
1979	Nottingham Forest	1975	Bayern Munich

European Cup-Winners Cup

1994	Arsenal	1984	Juventus
1993	Parma	1983	Aberdeen
1992	Werden Bremen	1982	Barcelona
1991	Manchester United	1981	Dinamo Tblisi
1990	Sampdoria	1980	Valencia
1989	Barcelona	1979	Barcelona
1988	Mechelan	1978	Anderlecht
1987	Ajax Amsterdam	1977	S. V. Hamburg
1986	Dynamo Kiev	1976	Anderlecht
1985	Everton	1975	Dynamo Kiev

European Championship

1992	Denmark	1972	West Germany
1988	Holland	1968	Italy
1984	France	1964	Spain
1980	West Germany	1960	USSR
1976	Czechoslovakia		

World Cup

1994	Brazil 0, Italy 0
	(Brazil won 3–2 on a penalty shoot-out after extra time)
1990	West Germany 1, Argentina 0
1986	Argentina 3, West Germany 2
1982	Italy 3, West Germany 1
1978	Argentina 3, Holland 1 (after extra time)
1974	West Germany 2, Holland 1
1970	Brazil 4, Italy 1

1966	England 4, West Germany 2
1962	Brazil 3, Czechoslovakia 1
1958	Brazil 5, Sweden 2
1954	West Germany 3, Hungary 2
1950	Uruguay 2, Brazil 1
1938	Italy 4, Hungary 2
1934	Italy 2, Czechoslovakia 1
1930	Uruguay 4, Argentina 2

UEFA Cup

1994	Inter Milan	1984	Tottenham
1993	Juventus	1983	Anderlecht
1992	Ajax Amsterdam	1982	IFK Gothenburg
1991	Inter Milan	1981	Ipswich
1990	Juventus	1980	Eintracht Frankfurt
1989	Napoli	1979	Bor. Moenchengladbach
1988	Bayer Leverkeusen	1978	P. S. V. Eindhoven
1987	IFK Gothenburg	1977	Juventus
1986	Real Madrid	1976	Liverpool
1985	Real Madrid	1975	Bor. Moenchengladbach

Rugby Union
International Championship

1994	Wales	1985	Ireland
1993	France	1984	Scotland
1992	England	1983	France and Ireland
1991	England	1982	Ireland
1990	Scotland	1981	France
1989	France	1980	England
1988	France and Wales	1979	Wales
1987	France	1978	Wales
1986	France and Scotland	1977	France

World Cup

| 1991 | Australia 12, England 6 |
| 1987 | New Zealand 29, France 9 |

Motor Racing

Formula One World Drivers Championship

1993	Alain Prost (France)
1992	Nigel Mansell (UK)
1991	Ayrton Senna (Brazil)
1990	Ayrton Senna (Brazil)
1989	Alain Prost (France)
1988	Ayrton Senna (Brazil)
1987	Nelson Piquet (Brazil)
1986	Alain Prost (France)
1985	Alain Prost (France)
1984	Niki Lauda (Austria)
1983	Nelson Piquet (Brazil)
1982	Keke Rosberg (Finland)
1981	Nelson Piquet (Brazil)
1980	Alan Jones (Australia)
1979	Jody Scheckter (S. Africa)
1978	Mario Andretti (USA)
1977	Niki Lauda (Austria)
1976	James Hunt (UK)
1975	Niki Lauda (Austria)
1974	Emerson Fittipaldi (Brazil)
1973	Jackie Stewart (UK)
1972	Emerson Fittipaldi (Brazil)
1971	Jackie Stewart (UK)
1970	Jochen Rindt (Austria)
1969	Jackie Stewart (UK)

1968	Graham Hill (UK)
1967	Denny Hulme (New Zealand)
1966	Jack Brabham (Australia)
1965	Jim Clark (UK)
1964	John Surtees (UK)
1963	Jim Clark (UK)
1962	Graham Hill (UK)
1961	Phil Hill (USA)
1960	Jack Brabham (Australia)
1959	Jack Brabham (Australia)
1958	Mike Hawthorn (UK)
1957	Juan Manuel Fangio (Argentina)
1956	Juan Manuel Fangio (Argentina)
1955	Juan Manuel Fangio (Argentina)
1954	Juan Manuel Fangio (Argentina)
1953	Alberto Ascari (Italy)
1952	Alberto Ascari (Italy)
1951	Juan Manuel Fangio (Argentina)
1950	Guiseppe Farina (Italy)

World Champions

Darts

1993	John Lowe (England)
1992	Phil Taylor (England)
1991	Dennis Priestley (England)
1990	Phil Taylor (England)
1989	Jocky Wilson (Scotland)
1988	Bob Anderson (England)
1987	John Lowe (England)
1986	Eric Bristow (England)
1985	Eric Bristow (England)
1984	Eric Bristow (England)

1983	Keith Deller (England)
1982	Jocky Wilson (Scotland)
1981	Eric Bristow (England)
1980	Eric Bristow (England)
1979	John Lowe (England)
1978	Leighton Rees (Wales)

Snooker

1994	Stephen Hendry (Scotland)
1993	Stephen Hendry (Scotland)
1992	Stephen Hendry (Scotland)
1991	John Parrott (England)
1990	Stephen Hendry (Scotland)
1989	Steve Davis (England)
1988	Steve Davis (England)
1987	Steve Davis (England)
1986	Joe Johnson (England)
1985	Dennis Taylor (N. Ireland)
1984	Steve Davis (England)
1983	Steve Davis (England)
1982	Alex Higgins (N. Ireland)
1981	Steve Davis (England)
1980	Cliff Thorborn (Canada)
1979	Terry Griffiths (Wales)
1978	Ray Reardon (Wales)
1977	John Spencer (England)
1976	Ray Reardon (Wales)
1975	Ray Reardon (Wales)
1974	Ray Reardon (Wales)
1973	Ray Reardon (Wales)
1972	Alex Higgins (N. Ireland)
1971	John Spencer (England)
1970	Ray Reardon (Wales)

Cricket World Cup Winners

1991	Pakistan	1979	West Indies
1987	Australia	1975	West Indies
1983	India		

American Sports

Football (Super Bowl)

1994	Dallas Cowboys	1980	Pittsburgh Steelers
1993	Dallas Cowboys	1979	Pittsburgh Steelers
1992	Washington Redskins	1978	Dallas Cowboys
1991	New York Giants	1977	Oakland Raiders
1990	San Francisco 49ers	1976	Pittsburgh Steelers
1989	San Francisco 49ers	1975	Pittsburgh Steelers
1988	Washington Redskins	1974	Miami Dolphins
1987	New York Giants	1973	Miami Dolphins
1986	Chicago Bears	1972	Dallas Cowboys
1985	San Francisco 49ers	1971	Baltimore Colts
1984	Los Angeles Raiders	1970	Kansas City Chiefs
1983	Washington Redskins	1969	New York Jets
1982	San Francisco 49ers	1968	Green Bay Packers
1981	Oakland Raiders	1967	Green Bay Packers

Baseball (World Series)

1993	Toronto Blue Jays (AL)
1992	Toronto Blue Jays (AL)
1991	Minnesota Twins (AL)
1990	Cincinnati Reds (NL)
1989	Oakland Athletics (AL)
1988	Los Angeles Dodgers (NL)
1987	Minnesota Twins (AL)
1986	New York Mets (NL)
1985	Kansas City Royals (AL)

1984	Detroit Tigers (AL)
1983	Baltimore Orioles (AL)
1982	St Louis Cardinals (NL)
1981	Los Angeles Dodgers (NL)
1980	Philadelphia Phillies (NL)

Olympic Venues

Summer Olympics

XXVII	2000	Sydney, Australia
XXVI	1996	Atlanta, USA
XXV	1992	Barcelona, Spain
XXIV	1988	Seoul, South Korea
XXIII	1984	Los Angeles, USA
XXII	1980	Moscow, USSR
XXI	1976	Montreal, Canada
XX	1972	Munich, Germany
XIX	1968	Mexico City, Mexico
XVIII	1964	Tokyo, Japan
XVII	1960	Rome, Italy
XVI	1956	Melbourne, Australia
XV	1952	Helsinki, Finland
XIV	1948	London, England
XIII	1944*	London, England
XII	1940*	Tokyo, then Helsinki
XI	1936	Berlin, Germany
X	1932	Los Angeles, USA
IX	1928	Amsterdam, Netherlands
VIII	1924	Paris, France
VII	1920	Antwerp, Belgium
VI	1916*	Berlin, Germany
V	1912	Stockholm, Sweden
IV	1908	London, England

	1906#	Athens, Greece
III	1904	St Louis, USA
II	1900	Paris, France
I	1896	Athens, Greece

* Cancelled due to World Wars

\# Intercalated Games to celebrate ten years of the Modern Olympics

Winter Olympics

XVIII	1998	Negano, Japan
XVII	1994	Lillehammer, Norway
XVI	1992	Albertville, France
XV	1988	Calgary, Canada
XIV	1984	Sarajevo, Yugoslavia
XIII	1980	Lake Placid, USA
XII	1976	Innsbruck, Austria
XI	1972	Sapporo, Japan
X	1968	Grenoble, France
IX	1964	Innsbruck, Austria
VIII	1960	Squaw Valley, USA
VII	1956	Cortina d'Ampezzo, Italy
VI	1952	Oslo, Norway
V	1948	St Moritz, Switzerland
IV	1936	Garmisch-Parten, Germany
III	1932	Lake Placid, USA
II	1928	St Moritz, Switzerland
I	1924	Chamonix, France

Commonwealth Games Venues

1994   Victoria, Canada

1990   Auckland, New Zealand

1986   Edinburgh, Scotland

1982   Brisbane, Australia